FIRESIDE

The Life Insurance Conspiracy

MADE ELEMENTARY BY

Sherlock Holmes

by PETER SPIELMANN
and AARON ZELMAN

with special contributions by insurance
legal expert DEAN SHARP *former*
counsel and investigator for the
U.S. Senate Judiciary Committee's
Antitrust and Monopoly Subcommittee
hearings on life insurance

All artwork by DAN BURR *and* KEITH WARD

A FIRESIDE BOOK
PUBLISHED BY
Simon and Schuster

Designed by Irving Perkins
Manufactured in the United States of America
1   2   3   4   5   6   7   8   9   10

Library of Congress Cataloging in Publication Data
Spielmann, Peter.
    The life insurance conspiracy.
    (A Fireside book)
    Edition published in 1976 under title: Holmes and
Watson solve the almost perfect crime—life insurance.
    Bibliography: p.
    1. Insurance, Life—United States. I. Zelman,
Aaron, joint author. II. Title.
HG8951.S73   1978   368.3′2′00973   78-24175
ISBN 0–671–24377–2 Pbk.

Companies wishing to be listed
in future editions of this guide
must send their policies with
complete details to Aaron Zelman,
Spielmann-Zelman Publishing Co.,
Box 76, Milwaukee, Wisconsin 53201.

Permission to use Sherlock Holmes
and Dr. Watson characters granted
by the A. Conan Doyle estate.

ACKNOWLEDGMENTS

The authors wish to acknowledge the help of Selene Leibl, Donald K. Stevens and Normund W. Leas. Special thanks to Jean Carper, Philip M. Stern, Morton Mintz, Herb Jaffe, Ann McFeatters, and numerous insurance company executives and the independent agents who must remain anonymous. Extra gratitude to Ray Carroll, who put us in touch with the right publisher, and to Al Reuben, Linda Sunshine, Barbara Jackson, and Pauline Finkelstein of Simon and Schuster.

The authors have no economic interest in any
company mentioned in this book.

Tax rulings change periodically, so it is best
to check with your tax advisor
rather than rely solely on this book
as an exhaustive discussion of the tax policy.

This book is dedicated to the memory of Senator Philip A. Hart, whose struggles on behalf of consumers in the United States Senate will hopefully be taken up by others. Philip Hart's periodic attempts to break up the concentration of power in major corporations never met with success, but his hearings before the Senate Judiciary Committee's Subcommittee on Antitrust and Monopoly alerted many people to the dangerous concentration of wealth and power in the life insurance industry.

Hart once said that he believed that "no one is irreplaceable, that no one institution is all-important and that the guard should be changed with some regularity." Although Senator Hart can never be replaced, we can only hope that his ideas and aspirations will be carried through to completion by new hands.

Contents

I would say that anyone contemplating buying insurance, wondering how much and what kind to buy, would save much money and headache, to say nothing of the mind-baffling jargon and outright deception accompanying most insurance sales pitches. In addition, the book is written engagingly, considering how forbidding the subject is and its usual presentation. I can only congratulate you on a much-needed job of public enlightenment.

> —ARTHUR DARACK
> *Editor*
> *Consumer Digest Publications*

The authors have done a great service in providing honest and frank information concerning a subject which has too long been obscured to the general public. The style of the book makes it easily read, easily understood, and is presented in a very frank, factual, and fair manner. I feel that every family will benefit from the information gained in this book as it calls the consumer back to the purpose of life insurance, which is death protection and not savings.

> —JAMES R. UNDERWOOD
> *President*
> *National Institute of Christian Financial Planning*

Sherlock Holmes always aligned with the cause of higher justice and, like the true Victorian gentleman that he was, he believed in fair play and honest dealing. As a devoted Holmesian student, I am delighted that Messrs. Spielmann and Zelman have used Holmes and his dependable companion Watson in such an effective and accurate manner.

> —John Bennett Shaw
> *Owner and curator of the world's*
> *largest private collection of*
> *Holmes literature, and member of*
> *The Baker Street Irregulars*

Foreword

Over the years the greed and callousness of too many life insurance companies and their whole-life agents have contributed to one of the most scandalous conspiracies America has ever known.

As executive director of the largest consumer organization in the nation, Consumer Federation of America, I have long been aware of the complexity of most life insurance. My organization has continually tried to alert and educate the consumer, but with limited resources it has been an uphill battle. The publication of this incredibly easy to read book is certainly a major contribution toward effective consumer education.

The knowledge contained in this book *is dangerous*—not to the consumers who take complete advantage of the information they are *not* supposed to know, but to those in the life insurance industry who often confuse consumers for profit. Consumers are typically kept confused and in the dark on life insurance despite the fact that they want more product information from the industry. *U.S. News & World Report*'s 1978 "Study of American Opinion" found that the life insurance industry received "good" ratings on providing enough product information from only 19 percent of the public!

One extremely interesting point about this book is that some insurance agents who currently advocate term insurance may be upset if consumers do read it. The reason is simple. This book tells how to buy term insurance the cheapest way! It is wise for consumers to compare what they now own (if indeed they were even offered a term policy) with the rates and companies listed in the book. This book provides much-needed information which maximizes the ability of consumers to spend their money wisely and obtain the most protection at the lowest price.

—Kathleen F. O'Reilly
Executive Director
Consumer Federation of America

Introduction

While serving as counsel and investigator for the late Senator Philip Hart's hearings into the chicanery of the life insurance companies who write most of the policies in this country, I became very familiar with the contrived complexity of a type of policy called "whole life" or "cash value" or "ordinary life" insurance. The terms are interchangeable, but the message is the same. This is the most touted, most expensively advertised, and most wasteful kind of insurance to buy. The fact that it is the most often sold type of policy only underlined for us then, as now, the life insurance industry's abuse of its public trust, its manipulation of the public's ignorance, and even its mistreatment of its own captive agents. (Captive agents are employed by a single company to sell *its* products only.)

Today, as an independent life insurance broker—free to sell any kind of policy that best suits a consumer—as well as a practicing lawyer, I am made aware constantly of the cash-value life insurance "racket."

And I am convinced it is a racket, a scam not unlike the "sting" sort of confidence game whereby the agent leads the consumer to believe that he will get "something for nothing"—that his insurance will "cost him nothing in the long run." As in any confidence game, greed and ignorance propel the buyer into the deal. He must realize that if the insurance costs him nothing, surely somebody, somehow, must be paying for it. But so long as the buyer thinks somebody else is the sucker, he will sign up now, while the offer holds. Only too late, if ever, does the buyer discover that he, himself, has been the sucker.

15

What is amazing to me is that the public has allowed itself to be so exploited, and that its state and national elected representatives have permitted this exploitation to continue for so many generations. Hopefully, *The Life Insurance Conspiracy*, a clear and engaging explanation of the cash-value life insurance "racket," will aid the public and its legislators to overcome their apathy and tolerance for being fleeced.

This isn't the first consumer's guide to buying life insurance, nor will it be the last. It is unique, however, in being as delightfully entertaining as it is informative. It is a fair, frank, and witty appraisal of the subject and, for that reason alone, it has been a pure pleasure for me to be of assistance to the authors. I'm pleased and proud to have helped them produce an in-depth buyer's guide which will give the reader all the information he needs to get the best life insurance buy for his money.

Just to avoid any confusion, the reader should keep in mind that although Holmes and Watson lived in London during the late nineteenth century, the facts of the insurance business presented here are true, even today, in America. While Holmes and Watson are fictional, the Trupolitan Insurance type of company and agents like Abernathy are among us today, emptying the pockets of millions of people.

Thus, the reader can be entertained while learning how insurance companies (and his own insurance policy) operate to rob and impoverish him. Insurance agents and companies will be outraged by this book, and Holmes fanciers may be less than pleased. However, consumers can easily discover in this book a way to save themselves hundreds and thousands of dollars on their insurance coverage, and assure the financial welfare of their families, whether they live to retire or die prematurely.

While certain concessions have been made in order to work the true story of insurance into the plot, the characters of Holmes and Watson themselves have been presented with literary and historic accuracy right down to their habits and foibles.

Here, then, is *The Life Insurance Conspiracy*, beginning with *The Adventure of the Indiscreet Agent* . . . Read, learn and enjoy.

—DEAN SHARP

1
The Adventure of the
Indiscreet Agent

The hot sunlight of July beat down on London without mercy, unrelieved by even the slightest breeze. The glare from the cobblestones of Baker Street and the buildings across the way was nearly as intolerable as the sun overhead, driving me from the window in disgust. My holiday was not due for another month. Thoughts circulated through my head like the contents of a simmering stew, which my poor head seemed hot enough to rival. My engagement to Miss Mary Morstan was foremost in my mind, developing out of the unparalleled events chronicled in my story entitled *The Sign of the Four*. I still lacked the means to support her in proper comfort, as my practice consisted thus far of the remaining patients of the elderly doctor whose practice I had depleted my purse by purchasing.

More alarming, however, was the lassitude which had fallen over my friend Sherlock Holmes. While the heat drove me to wander ceaselessly about our lodgings, Holmes still occupied the divan where he had planted himself the night before. Stacks of newspaper clippings, heaps of pipe ashes, and the remains of dinner told me that Holmes had spent a restless night.

No new public or private cases had been recommended to his

Holmes still occupied the divan where he had planted himself the night before.

attention for weeks, and of all crises, inactivity was the most dangerous to Holmes. While on the track of a desperate criminal, Holmes fairly radiated energy, but a prolonged hiatus from his work as a consulting detective was wont to drive him to the needle. Already yesterday Holmes had been gazing on the veins of his forearm with a yearning I knew all too well. Today, I hoped, would bring a client to relieve his boredom.

"Good morning," I said. "It looks like we're in for another beastly day."

"Thank you for the observation," snapped Holmes. "I had already come to that conclusion."

"Really, Holmes," I answered brusquely, "you could at least begin the day in a more civil mood. This heat will end, you know, and so will the lapse in your clients."

"Ah, but when, Watson? That's the question. I've been combing the papers all night in search of unsolved cases, undetected patterns, clues, and dark motives. What do I find for my troubles? What are the events of the day, the talk of the town? 'MP Keeps Mistress in Soho Flat.' Titillating, but hardly unusual. 'London Woman Evicted; Kept 330 Pet Cats.' That's unusual enough, but not criminal. Even the 'agony' columns are nothing but blather and bleat recently, with lost dogs and gratitude for patron saints crowding the usual tales of missing lovers and secret rendezvous from the pages.

"No, Watson, I've outsmarted myself this time. I do believe that all the clever criminals have already either been rounded up or have fled London. Let us hope that one of the provincial counties will intervene to provide me with a case worthy of my mettle, or perhaps a recent immigrant will perpetrate some outrage to baffle the local police. They are getting remarkably fat and lazy since I've been assisting them unofficially."

"Really, Holmes," I answered, "your desires would seem quite perverse to one who knew you less well than I. Most people would be quite satisfied that London is peaceful presently, without yearning for another 'outrage,' as you put it."

"Well, Watson, my wishes may be motivated by idleness and a touch of selfishness. . . . Do I hear a hansom stopping at our door?

Look out the window like a good man, and tell me if this drought is about to be relieved."

Alighting from the carriage in front of our door was a well-dressed young man of about thirty, carrying bundles of notebooks and a small valise under his arms. Taking care not to drop his parcels, he screwed a monocle into his right eye, glanced over his wardrobe, and rang the bell for Mrs. Hudson.

"Ah! Our prayers are answered, Watson. Unless I'm mistaken, that bell heralds the advent of a new case. I suppose I'd better tidy up a bit." For Holmes, this meant pushing his heap of clippings under the divan and settling into his chair to reload his brier pipe, for his linen was always immaculate. He finished tamping the pipe and rose just as the sound of ascending footsteps reached our door, punctuated by two light taps outside.

"I'd better admit our visitor," Holmes said, "lest he drop his bundles and delay our inquiries into whatever problem he wishes to pose to me."

He spoke too soon, however, for the door opened on an avalanche of papers and books issuing from the overburdened arms of our guest. There were momentary glimpses of charts, graphs, and tables of figures as they cascaded from his arms to the hallway floor, revealing a chagrined young man blushing behind them.

"Welcome to our humble suite, Mr. Abernathy," said Holmes in greeting. "May I help you with your things?"

"Yes, thank you very— how do you know my name?" asked Mr. Abernathy, looking up with mouth agape as he hurriedly gathered his books to himself. "I was unannounced, and I don't recall our ever having met."

"The engraved plate on the handle of your valise, sir, proclaims your identity as plainly as any card ever did. You exposed the handle to me just now as you set it down to pick up your belongings. I believe that I have the advantage on you, however. My name is Mr. Sherlock Holmes, consulting detective by trade. May I be of assistance to you?"

"I'm in the right place then! I should have been so embarrassed otherwise. This gentleman, then, must be Dr. Watson, your biographer."

The door opened on an avalanche of papers and books issuing from the overburdened arms of our guest.

I smiled and nodded my greetings. "The same," said I.

"You are the very man I wish to see," said Abernathy, pumping my hand and spilling papers from a folder. "I cannot tell you how much I enjoyed your latest work which, quite frankly, filled me with awe of your detective friend Mr. ·Holmes." Holmes smiled and winked at me from behind the effusive Abernathy. "I was particularly interested to learn of your impending marriage— I trust I'm not too forward, my dear doctor, but you see it is my business to be aware of such matters."

"Just what is your line, Mr. Abernathy?" I asked.

"Why, insurance, Dr. Watson. I have assured the financial welfare and peace of mind of almost one hundred of your neighbors here in Baker Street and the surrounding area, and I would be remiss in my duty if I didn't inquire as to your own situation, knowing of your plan to take to yourself a wife. Forgive my being frank, Doctor, but being an avid reader of your stories, I couldn't help noticing your plans."

During this last exchange, the smile had evaporated from Holmes's face like butter placed in the broiling summer sun. He now slumped back into his easy chair by the fireplace, touched a match to his brier, and began to send billowing clouds of tobacco smoke to the ceiling in silence.

I beckoned Abernathy to another chair, and sat facing him.

"Being a doctor, you are aware of the fragility of life," began Abernathy. "Many persons are quite cognizant of the fact that our lives are fleeting at best, over before they are hardly begun. Indeed, so tenuous is the thread that binds together body and soul that it not uncommonly is prematurely cut, bearing the unfortunate individual to that land where the mundane earthly worries of food, shelter, and taxes no longer press upon him."

"Yes, Mr. Abernathy, I see such tragedies weekly," I replied, "but I'm sure you haven't come here to lecture me upon the fine points regarding mind-body duality. Kindly come to the point, as I must be off upon my rounds shortly."

"Certainly, my dear doctor. Once you have married Miss Morstan, you will feel yourself the master of your castle. Your home and practice will be established. You may even gain some celebrity from your literary efforts. Suddenly, in the midst of this prosperity, the most dire event occurs! Your Mary and children are suddenly left without you, and without the means to continue their style of life! Who is to care for them? Your family?"

"Well, no," I admitted. The remnants of the Watson family had long been scattered before the winds.

"Precisely, Doctor. Now, my company makes a habit of providing for the comfort of widows and children for the rest of their dependent lives, in exchange for a token monthly fee. By collecting a small amount from many thousands of people, we are able to make generous settlements with the widows of the unfortunate few who turn out to actually die before their productive days are over."

"Sounds more like death insurance than life insurance, eh, Holmes?"

"Would that death could be postponed so cheaply and easily, Watson," said Holmes dryly, drumming his fingers in impatience on the arm of his chair.

"Furthermore, Doctor," continued Abernathy, "it is now possible to buy insurance that will pay you if you live, as well as your survivors if you die prematurely. The pure death protection I just described is what we call 'term insurance,' because it is only good for the time period, or term, for which you have bought it. While it pays admirable benefits to your survivors, most people will never see those benefits because most wage earners actually outlive the term of the term insurance policy."

"That seems a pity, considering that most people have so little money to spare. They might be considered worth more dead than alive!" I said.

"That's precisely the way my company looks at the matter, Doctor. I must commend you on your quick perception, which seems quite the equal of your friend's. Really, you do no justice to your own abilities in your writings, Doctor," said Abernathy. I accepted the compliment with a smile and a nod, while Holmes sent a larger than usual cloud of smoke toward the ceiling.

"Now, Doctor, for the same monthly premium, my company will sell you a policy that we call 'whole-life insurance,' meaning that it is good for your whole life, or at least until you reach one hundred, which ought to be plenty of time. What we do is to open an 'account' for you which builds up cash values throughout the time you keep your insurance. If you die, your survivors receive the death benefit. If you live to retire, however, you will receive a generous cash settlement, equal to the cash value of your policy. Thus, you win whether you live or die! It's a genuine miracle, Dr. Watson! How could you possibly refuse such a policy?"

This last exchange had stirred Holmes out of his dejection. After tamping a fresh load of tobacco from the Persian slipper on the mantelpiece into his pipe, he approached Mr. Abernathy. "Tell me something, Mr. Abernathy. If my friend here dies insured by your 'miraculous' whole-life, cash-value policy, how much of a settlement will his bereaved widow receive?"

"Well, Mr. Holmes, it would be about ten thousand dollars."

"And if he were insured with your term insurance?"

"Well, we can't assume he'll die prematurely; most people don't, you know. Actually, his chances of death are rather remote, so his widow probably would never get that settlement."

"Just so, Mr. Abernathy. How much would Mrs. Watson stand to get under the term policy?"

"Well, that would depend on the term policy, Mr. Holmes. But it very well could be thirty thousand, or maybe forty thousand dollars, or possibly even more," said Abernathy haltingly, dropping his voice and blushing.

Holmes's eyes widened perceptibly, and the astonishingly large difference between the two benefits quite took my breath away.

"Tell me, my good fellow, why do you recommend to my friend the whole-life policy, which pays such paltry death benefits? When you came in, you quite distinctly spoke of the fleeting nature of mortality in an effort to convince the doctor of the need of providing emergency income for his survivors. Now you propose to leave them with a benefit that wouldn't last them a year, on the assumption the doctor won't meet an untimely fate. What is your real calling, Mr. Abernathy, insurance or investment?"

"Well, Mr. Holmes, there are good reasons why the death benefit should be smaller in the whole-life policy, which is a superior product. After all, in exchange for guaranteeing the insured a handsome nest egg to retire on, we could hardly be expected to hand out such lavish death benefits in addition."

"Mr. Abernathy, the death benefit you give to the whole-life customer is not only less than 'lavish,' it is downright inadequate to meet the needs of the widowed Mrs. Watson. Really, you hardly inspire confidence in your product or your advice if you propose to have the doctor pay you for inadequate insurance protection on the assumption he won't perish anyway. Why should he buy insurance at all in that case? Why shouldn't he take the same money and save or invest it? He would then have his nest egg without your advice."

"He could hardly be guaranteed of receiving his investment, yet our company always pays our beneficiaries if they keep up their insurance."

"By the same token, banks are just as safe. What is the rate of interest my friend would receive on his 'cash values'?"

"My charts show that over the years, Dr. Watson would gain four percent before taxes on his 'cash values.' "

Sherlock Holmes broke out into a hearty laugh at that information. "Why, Mr. Abernathy, the savings institutions pay five to eight percent from the time you walk in the door! Perhaps we'd better change the subject, though. I'm sure there must be other compensating features that make this 'whole-life' insurance as attractive and miraculous as you claim."

"There certainly are," said Abernathy, who appeared to be affronted at my friend's ribbing. "Should Dr. Watson be in need of funds, he could borrow the monies in his cash-value account back from the company; thus he has access to his money whenever he wants."

"You say 'borrow,' Mr. Abernathy," said I. "Surely you must mean 'withdraw.' Borrowing usually connotes the payment of interest on a loan, and I assume I wouldn't have to pay your company interest to withdraw my own money from this account?"

"On the contrary, Doctor, you would be required to pay the company eight percent interest on the money you borrowed. That's the way the company encourages its clients to keep their funds in their cash-value accounts so that the company can invest those funds."

"My dear Mr. Abernathy, you do yourself a disservice," remarked

Holmes. "You entered our flat prepared to offer the doctor a wonderful service, and then you switch his attention to another product which combines the worst features of insurance and investments. You propose to sign him up for a policy which pays small death benefits to his widow if he dies, and a meager sum on retirement if he lives to collect it. Furthermore, you propose to charge him interest to use what you call his own money! It's very clear that once the doctor turns his money over to you, it becomes the company's money, which he can only borrow at a high rate of interest!"

During this last exchange, Mr. Abernathy began to perspire even more freely than before, and his tongue darted out to moisten his lips repeatedly. "Really, Mr. Holmes, I don't understand why you show me unwonted hostility! I'm simply trying to assure that the doctor's financial affairs are in order for the new phase of life he intends to enter. I don't like to dwell on death. I'm really a life-

"Really, Mr. Holmes, I don't understand why you show me unwonted hostility!" Mr. Abernathy complained. "I only want to see that the doctor has some protection."

loving person. Indeed, I am. I only want to see that the doctor has some protection, and funds to retire on."

"Mr. Abernathy, it's quite plain that although you have noble aims," I replied, "you cloak yourself with suspicion when you try to divert my attention away from death protection to your inferior 'whole-life' policy. Do you really think me that inattentive? Mr. Holmes and I have some little reputation for observation, you know."

"Quite so, my dear Watson," Holmes added. "Tell me, sir, is this your first position after leaving Cambridge?"

At this, Mr. Abernathy sank into a chair in amazement. "Mr. Holmes, I do believe you are the devil himself! How did you peg me out as a university man?"

"A childishly simple deduction, almost as elementary as the observation that you've shaken off a severe summer cold, Mr. Abernathy."

Holmes's non-explanation astounded me as much as Abernathy; I could see from his bearing and from the fraternity ring upon his hand that the agent was an educated man, but the deduction of illness caught me quite off guard. "Holmes, a fresh illustration of your powers certainly doesn't explain your first inference; I confess I'm as puzzled as Abernathy. It is true you've suffered an illness, then, sir?"

"Yes, I have, Dr. Watson, but it's clean beyond me how you figured that out, Mr. Holmes! I've had no symptoms for two days now, and I think I've completely recovered."

Holmes chuckled heartily at our mutual amazement. "My dear Mr. Abernathy, the fact is quite as plain as the nose on your face. The chapped and peeling condition of the skin about your nostrils informed me that you've been blowing your nose inordinately recently, indicating either illness or allergy. As you've had no breathing difficulties since you entered our apartment, I deduced a cold. Obviously, an allergy would leave you still gasping and sneezing in this pollen season. That, combined with the knowledge that last week was unseasonably cold and wet—and your boots still show signs of watermarks—practically puts the matter beyond a doubt! As to your university, the colors in your necktie and your university ring are as unmistakable as a gown and mortarboard to the trained observer. Now that I've answered your questions, Mr. Abernathy, perhaps you'd be kind enough to tell me one or two things before your departure."

"Well, within reason, surely."

"Have you been in this profession of yours long, Mr. Abernathy?"

"Why no, Mr. Holmes, just six months now."

"Have you found sales to be difficult?"

"Not at first, but then I was mostly dealing with my family, friends, acquaintances, university fellows, fraternity brothers, and others who know me. More recently, however, I find I must contact complete strangers, and my home office is closely watching me, for my productivity has fallen markedly."

"Have you noticed a similar tendency in other of your fellow agents?"

"Now that you mention it, you're correct. There are several men there who have been in the business for years, but they have large, reliable accounts. They rarely make new sales, but simply mind the office, take the pick of the clients who approach us, and look down their noses on us commissioned agents."

"Oh, you receive a commission rather than salary? Tell me, is the commission for the 'term insurance' you introduced the same as for the 'whole-life' insurance you tried to then sell the good doctor?"

At this question, Abernathy's newly recovered composure again evaporated, and he blushed deeply. "Actually, no, Mr. Holmes."

"I thought as much," interjected Holmes. "Isn't it true your commission on the whole-life policy is rather higher than on the term policy, Mr. Abernathy?"

"I won't deny it, Mr. Holmes, but that's none of my doing. I've sometimes wondered about that myself, but I can't afford to go questioning my employer about these matters. When I brought the subject up once, my branch manager explained to me again the marvelous advantages of the whole-life policy and its retirement plan, and I didn't dare to challenge his word. After all, I've got to feed my family, same as everyone else. I can't afford to stir up antagonism in my office."

"No one will deny you the right to your daily bread, Mr. Abernathy, but do take care that you're not taking it out of the mouths

"Why didn't you call a constable?" I asked Holmes. "This man is obviously selling fraudulent goods."

of others, and in doing so, making them destitute. Good day to you, sir. I don't think we'll be needing any life insurance today," said Holmes while opening the door to our guest.

As the nonplussed Abernathy made his retreat, I asked Holmes, "Why didn't you call a constable? This man is obviously selling fraudulent goods; this matter ought to be investigated!"

"Calm yourself, old fellow. This Abernathy is merely the agent of a higher power. Detaining him would have done no good. Can't you see he's merely the prisoner of circumstance? His superiors have meticulously trained him into believing in his wares, and he can't afford to exercise his own intelligence to reason out the part he is playing. No, my dear Watson, this is quite a three-pipe problem. I ask your indulgence while I think this puzzle out."

I begged my leave and proceeded to attend to my patients. Early in the evening, I returned to Baker Street to find Holmes engaged in laying out various costumes and disguises, selecting a new identity for some role he was to play.

"Greetings again, Watson." He smiled. "I believe that I see a way to penetrate the workings of the Trupolitan Insurance Company, which employs the hapless Mr. Abernathy. During your absence, I made my way to his home office in a suitable disguise and, posing as an out-of-work accountant with brown hair and tinted spectacles, managed to find employment as a life insurance agent for his very own company.

"During my interview, the luckless Abernathy returned from his afternoon calls and was summoned straight away to the branch manager's office. He emerged looking considerably depressed; I suspect he will not remain in their employ long, which is probably all for the better. He seems an honest enough sort at heart, but he's currently enmeshed in a criminal conspiracy which is so vast that I can only dimly conceive of its power and wealth! By the way, Abernathy looked directly at me, perhaps seeing in me his replacement, but failed to penetrate my disguise." Holmes smiled.

I chuckled knowingly; long experience had made me familiar with Holmes's expertise in the use of disguises. On numerous occasions in the past, he had tricked me, his very roommate, into mistaking him for an asthmatic sea captain or a nonconformist clergyman. "So then," I said, "have you unraveled the plot to sell me overly expensive insurance already? I've only been absent some five hours now."

"No, Watson, not entirely, but the whole affair begins to take shape. By paying their agents on a commission basis, and rewarding them more highly for pushing the grossly inferior 'whole-life' insurance policies on people, this insurance company has skimmed untold billions off the working people of our land. What I need to discover is whether this practice is widespread, whether other devious practices are used by these life insurance companies, and who is at the back of it. I'm afraid I'll be no company to you for the next few days, as I'll be out learning this business in disguise, or here waiting to receive a procession of agents from various companies. No, Watson, unless you wish to be bored to tears with actuarial tables and talk of dividends, annuities, endowments, retirement benefits, cash-surrender values, and other esoteric insurance terms, you'll spend your next few days courting Miss Morstan, and allow me to serve as your insurance investigator."

So I followed his advice, and put the whole affair out of my mind for three days. During that time, I stopped in our lodgings only late in the evening to sleep, and Holmes invariably returned later and rose earlier than I. Mrs. Hudson, however, informed me that during the past days a whole succession of young men carrying briefcases, valises, charts, graphs, and even one with a small blackboard had ascended the seventeen steps to our rooms during the daytime. These, I assumed, were the agents Holmes questioned, with perhaps Holmes himself in some disguise. I was curious as to what results my friend was discovering, but I knew that he would call upon me when he needed my services and would give explanations only after all the loose ends of a case were tied up.

That didn't occur until that Friday night, while I rested my weary legs after an unusually long and busy day. I was perusing the latest issue of *The Lancet* when I heard measured, stately footsteps coming up our stairway. Knocks sounded at the door, and I opened it to admit a tall, thin, bespectacled gentleman overburdened with books, notebooks, and other bundles and papers. It required close inspection to see beneath the false hairpiece, glasses, mustache, and vaguely ill-fitting clothing the figure of my friend. Holmes walked into his bedroom without a word, reappearing ten minutes later looking once again youthful and well groomed.

He stalked the length of our sitting room again and again, his brows knitted together in thought, his hands buried in his pockets. Holmes picked up one of the books he had brought home, which seemed to be a loosely bound manual of some kind. *Training Manual for Agents,* I read on the cover when I glimpsed it.

With a sudden outburst, Holmes hurled the booklet into the fireplace and cursed it. He then sank into his favorite chair and reached out for his pipe and matches. He lit his favorite brier pipe with his first match; then he struck another, and tossed it onto the *Training Manual.* When the pages began to blacken and curl back, revealing a bewildering array of graphs and charts, a smile creased his face and he began to laugh heartily.

2

The Conspiracy Unraveled

"Well, Watson, by now you must be quite eager to hear the results of my investigations," he finally said.

"I have been very curious."

"My dear friend and doctor, had I not been here to confound Abernathy with my unexpected questions, you most probably would have been added to the long, long list of people who have been defrauded by the Trupolitan Insurance Company, and if not by Trupolitan, by one or another of the eighteen hundred or so companies now preying upon the death fears and ignorance of the public.

"In the first place, the training that agents like Mr. Abernathy receive is as minimal as their expertise; I became a licensed insurance agent the day after Mr. Abernathy visited us."

"You! An insurance agent!" I couldn't believe my ears.

"Yes, Watson, and you needn't look so astonished. After my first visit to Trupolitan, I dropped in on an independent insurance agent, one who represents many different companies. I learned that licensing tests for insurance agents are held weekly, and that very afternoon they would be testing in a neighboring city. He gave me some books and pamphlets to study. I looked them over on the train ride, and I passed the test with flying colors. From this, I learned that any clever person can become an insurance agent without any particular experience in the field.

"My next stop was at the stall of Murphy, the Tottenham Court book vendor. There, amidst his musty tomes of obsolete knowledge, I exhumed this little-known import," said Holmes, pulling a slim brown volume from his stack of books.

"*Traps Baited with Orphans*, by Elizur Wright, published in 1877," he read. "This is a marvelous little classic which has gone unnoticed in England. Wright is from America, was a mathematician and minister's son, and became the first insurance commissioner of Massachusetts. His book explores and exposes the fallacy of trying to use life insurance as an investment in the way young Abernathy tried to 'sell' you, Watson. Wright was a perceptive critic of the industry he tried to regulate. He coined the maxim 'I became convinced that life insurance was the most available, convenient, and permanent breeding place for rogues that civilization had ever presented.' He was right. Furthermore, there has been no material change in conditions since he wrote that. You will say so yourself as soon as you understand what Abernathy was trying to sell you.

"I also found on Murphy's shelves a fragmentary reference to an American actuary named Sheppard Homans, from 1868, when he declared, 'There is but one function for the institution of life insurance, and that is protection. The insurance Companies are introducing a savings feature which, while it increases the cost of insurance, does not increase the protection.'

"Lomax, the sub-librarian of the British Museum, was my next informant. He retreated into the aisles of the library, and returned with the first reference to life insurance in England he could find. It was not a story to inspire confidence in the motives of insurers, Watson; quite the contrary. The first life insurance contract Lomax could retrieve was contested by the insurers, who attempted to break the contract.

"It's an old story, and an unfortunately common one. It underlines the fact that business arrangements should not be contracted over ale in a public house. Back on June 18, 1536, a certain William Gybbons was imbibing with some friends at the Old Drury Ale House. Gybbons was not old or ill, and seemed destined to attain a comfortable old age. His friends, however, perhaps aided by a few rounds of ale, convinced William Gybbons that they would pay his survivor two thousand dollars if he died within the coming year—if Gybbons paid them eighty dollars as a premium. Gybbons accepted the offer, and the first recorded life insurance contract was in force.

"Undoubtedly Gybbons' 'friends' had a fine time drinking up his premium money and telling other alehouse cronies how they had profited by betting on an apparently sure thing.

"They must have been greatly dismayed when William Gybbons passed away slightly less than one year later, on May twenty-ninth. Dismayed, but not disarmed, his friends decided that they would not pay his beneficiary the two thousand dollars they owed, and this brought the whole sordid affair to the notice of the courts, and into the realm of written history.

"Gybbons' friends argued that they had intended the term of 'one year' to mean one *lunar* year of twelve months, each month being made up of twenty-eight days. Under this understanding, Gybbons had outlived the policy on May twentieth, 1537, and they had no obligation to pay up.

"Unfortunately for them, they hadn't put this in writing in Gybbons' policy, and the court rejected their argument. The two thousand dollars was paid, and insurance companies have been doing their best to avenge that setback since then.

"Today, however, they have acquired the sophistication of hundreds of years of experience, and fleece the public with so deft a touch that their expropriations generally go unnoticed.

"My patron company, Trupolitan, has two main insurance products to offer the public. The simplest is their term insurance, which anyone can understand in an instant. You simply pay the company an annual fee, and they will pay your survivor a large sum of money if you die during the time period in which you are insured. It's very much like the fire insurance on your offices, Watson; you only rent the term insurance for the time you've ordered it from the company.

"Due to human biology, however, it costs the company more to insure your life as you grow older. This is simply because the older you are the less likely it is you will live to see the next year. The insurance company passes along the cost of this extra risk to you,

34

so if you want the same amount of protection, you must be willing to pay more each year. This is called 'level term' insurance, and I shall return to it in a moment.

"Most people, however, don't need the same amount of insurance every year. When they are young, they generally need a great deal of insurance to guarantee that there will be enough money to raise their children and keep their widow in comfort; as they get older, however, less money is needed because the children are growing up and the expense of raising them has already been paid. By the time children leave home to care for themselves, not as much insurance is needed. All you need do then, Watson, is tell the company to reduce the amount of protection.

"All insurance companies have term insurance, but those that specialize in it offer several types to fit the needs and wishes of people in different circumstances. Besides the 'decreasing term' insurance which I have just described, they offer 'level term' insurance, which I mentioned a moment ago. Here the death benefit does not decrease, though of course the cost gradually rises with your age. Companies that sincerely want to help the consumers will make these policies available to age one hundred. Companies like Trupolitan don't find them profitable enough for their tastes, so they cut them off at age sixty or sixty-five. Then they have the unmitigated gall to claim that you can't get term insurance after age sixty-five! This is one of the commonest lies that insurance agents learn by rote to recite to every prospective buyer they meet. I wager that not one in a thousand insurance agents is even aware that term insurance is available after age sixty-five! They only know their own company doesn't offer it, so they make the deductive leap to the assumption that no company offers it. That is, if they think at all. Insurance companies prefer agents whose brains are wholly given over to memorizing sales manuals, with no cells left over for original thought or analysis.

"Not only is term insurance very good for the consuming public, but an insurance company and its agents can make a very comfortable profit by selling this type of protection. The proof of that is that there are a handful of companies that specialize in low-cost term insurance, and they have been in existence for many years."

"If that's so, Holmes, then what is the meaning of this 'whole-life' insurance that Abernathy attempted to sell me?"

"Ah, now you've put your finger on the fraud. This 'whole-life' insurance is nothing more or less than a very small term insurance policy combined with a dreadfully bad savings account of sorts that pays off quite meagerly when you retire. It works this way:

"When you buy such a policy, the agent may not tell you that if you die, your widow will receive only the death benefit listed on the face of the policy. For example, Watson, if you had purchased Mr. Abernathy's ten-thousand-dollar policy and had died after putting in five thousand dollars of your own, your widow would only receive the ten-thousand-dollar death benefit. Just what this *really* means in the long run you'll see in a moment. Right now, it's enough for you to know that your five thousand dollars, or cash values, which many people mistakenly think of as a 'savings account,' are absorbed—or as the actuaries would say, are 'merged'—into the death benefit of the policy when you die. In fact, you have no 'personal account' with the insurance company; your money is thrown into the company's vault with everybody else's, to be used for investment, for agents' commissions, for expensive vacations for profitable agents, or any other good 'investments' which Trupolitan sees fit to make. If you decide to borrow your cash values back from the Trupolitan, you'll find out just what kind of an 'account' you have. First, you may have to wait up to *six months* before you can even receive your money; that's to protect the company from reckless borrowers like yourself, my dear doctor. Then you'll have to pay the Trupolitan Company interest on the loan— interest on what the smiling agent referred to as 'your own money'— in 'your own account'!

"But if you leave the money in Trupolitan's hands, they will pay you interest on it. Oh yes, and very generous they are about it, too; they'll pay you less interest than any other possible investment you could make, unless you sewed it up in your mattress. The interest they pay you is *so* sub-marginal that it even fails to keep up with increases in your cost of living, so that over the years your money becomes worth less and less. In a real sense, you are losing part of the value of your money while the insurance company holds it, even though they may give you some interest on it in order to make the sale in the first place.

"You see that what you really get with 'whole life' is an either/or insurance and investment program. If you die, you get the insurance and nothing more; you lose the cash values. If you live, you get the paltry cash values, but the insurance then expires instead of you."

"But Holmes, if I die and receive the death benefit, isn't part of that death benefit that my widow gets really a return on my own savings?"

"Now you've hit upon it, Watson! I really underestimate you sometimes. Yes, you pay a level insurance premium for decreasing death protection plus extra money that goes into your cash values; if you die, the cash values make up for the decreased amount of insurance you are buying. Actually, you are insuring yourself for that amount. As each year goes by, the company is giving you less and less insurance protection. For example, if you buy a twenty-thousand-dollar policy, and after ten years your cash values are built up to five thousand dollars, then when you die, your widow receives five thousand in cash values plus only fifteen thousand in insurance protection. In this way, you are providing your own insurance. I've brought back a chart which should make the matter perfectly clear. (See page 38.)

"As you can see, Watson, the very first year is the only time when you are really getting the whole twenty thousand dollars in insurance protection. As time passes, more and more of that death benefit consists of your own slowly accumulated cash values. In fact, you can find out just how much insurance you are getting by subtracting the cash values from the death benefit on the face of the policy. You can see from the chart that by age sixty-five you are really getting fifteen thousand dollars in insurance, not twenty thousand dollars, since the other five thousand dollars of the death benefit is your own money! Now, this system wouldn't be so bad if the death benefits were larger, but they are not."

"Holmes," I asked, "why did that scoundrel Abernathy attempt to sell me this expensive whole-life policy when he well knew how low the death benefit paid to Mary would be?"

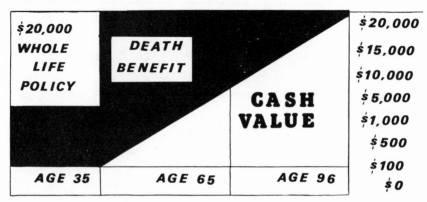

"Your insurance disappears as your cash values rise," Holmes pointed out with the help of his chart.

"Now, now, Watson, you must not blame the poor agent too much. His behavior is completely predictable and explicable when you realize that his first-year commission for selling term insurance is thirty-five to sixty percent while his first-year commission on whole-life is all of fifty-five to seventy percent. With such a differ-ence in commission, *plus the fact that the whole-life costs much more,* few agents, particularly the newcomers to the profession, can resist pushing whole-life insurance on people, even when they know for a fact that term insurance is cheaper and provides a bigger death benefit. I suspect that if the Trupolitan and other insurance companies rewarded agents equally for selling whole-life and term insurance, we would see much more term insurance being sold. Human nature is frail enough in the best of circumstances, so we shouldn't be surprised to see agents succumb to economic tempta-tions. In addition, Watson, the insurance companies harass and penalize agents who sell term insurance.

"While making my rounds to sell people insurance, I fully ex-plained both policies to them and they always chose the term policy. Those people who were a little more affluent and wanted a more secure future also asked about other investments which would give them comfort and financial security in their retirement at a much greater rate of growth than a whole-life policy. When fully informed of the nature of the two policies, not one of my 'clients' over the past three days freely chose the whole-life over the term insurance. Yet the Trupolitan and most other insurance companies sell many, many more whole-life than term policies. Why? Because the agents confuse the issue and push them on people. Why do the agents do that? Because the company rewards them more highly for selling the whole-life. Why does the company want that? Because then the insurance company can gather to itself all those lovely cash values—your hard-earned money, Watson—and invest them and make money for itself!

"Just walk through the business section of any major city, Watson. Who has the biggest and most expensive, the most glamorous and costly, the tallest and most spacious buildings? Why, the institutions with the most money: the insurance companies and the banks. In many cities, the insurance companies virtually compete with each other to see who can erect the most costly edifice. And when they've put up their buildings, they turn to real estate ventures, the stock exchange, even buying out other insurance companies and

"People buy whole-life insurance instead of term because the agents push it on them," Holmes said grimly.

banks—anywhere to secrete the mountains of money they've wrung out of the public by their unconscionable overcharges. Even if they aren't legally or technically guilty of theft, they are morally guilty.

"Some insurance companies, however, are not content even with this extra income. These are the mutual insurance companies, which are the real giants of the industry. Mutual companies do not have stockholders who have invested money in them, as most companies do. The word 'mutual' suggests that the company is mutually owned by the policyholders, and the policyholders of the company are under the impression that they elect the officers of the company, who elect the board of directors. In actual practice, this turns out to be utter rubbish!

"The mutual companies have spread the false notion that since the policyholders own the company they share in the profits of the company. These 'shared profits' supposedly come to the policyholder in the form of 'dividends,' which the company pays whenever it can afford to. These supposed 'dividends' are not dividends in the usual sense of the word, however. What the mutual companies do is raise the cost of the policy another thirty percent on the average, thus getting that much extra money out of the pocket of the poor insurance buyer. They then invest this extra money, just as the individual could if he cared to, and later split the earnings on their investments between the policyowner and themselves.

"The 'dividends' the policyholder finally gets back, however, are nothing more than his own money—extra money he needlessly paid to the company for them to invest. The proof of this is that true dividends are considered taxable income; the tax collector demands his percentage on any real dividends. Insurance company 'dividends,' however, are recognized by the tax collector as nothing more than a partial refund of the overpayment on the policy by the policyholder, and thus should not be and are not taxed. But the company, when it pays out dividends, can deduct them from its income tax!

"Many insurance agents represent these 'dividends' as a share in the company's profits, which they are not. This is a deceptive sales practice which many agents indulge in. Even when they do not explicitly call these refunds 'dividends,' the agents leave the clear impression that is what they are. There are laws against this practice, but violations of the law are almost never reported, because the public is uninformed.

"Usually, the company does repay these 'dividends' to the customer; however, the company is not required to repay, and sometimes does not. If the rate of payment were better, these 'dividends' might justify themselves, but they do not. The fact is, an individual can invest that extra thirty percent overcharge himself and get a much better profit on it, even after paying taxes. By the way, as proof that these 'dividends' are merely overcharges, I submit this advertisement for your consideration.

To Our Policyholders

The Company on November 25, 1918, had paid in policy claims $14,000,000 more than to the corresponding date in 1917; and claims in the ordinary department are still being received in double the normal number daily. The claims in the ordinary department are proportionately greater in number than in the industrial department. The extraordinary claim payments are due to the epidemic of influenza and have more than used up the amount tentatively set aside for the distribution of dividends in 1919. *We regret to announce that the Board of Directors has been constrained to omit the usual declaration of dividends upon policies in the ordinary department. The holders of the policies issued on our non-participatory plan may congratulate themselves that the low premiums charged gave them these dividends in advance.*

The Metropolitan Life Insurance Company

"Therefore, on top of the basic term policy, which is the essence of all these insurance policies, the companies add the extra cost of the cash-value scheme, and the mutual companies add the further cost of this extra refundable investment fee. The saddest part is that this is the type of policy sold to the majority of people, who usually lack the education to see through this fraud.

"Topping the whole scheme off is the usual practice of the mutual insurance company agent who persuades the client to take his 'dividends' after they are available and use them to buy more insurance, which he calls 'paid-up additions.' The cruel fraud involved in this is that the client gets only a pitifully small amount of insurance for his money this way. For example, at age thirty-five, a client could buy about three dollars' worth of cash-value insurance for every dollar of 'dividend' he uses for this purpose. The absurdity of this becomes apparent when you realize that the same dollar could buy him about three hundred dollars' worth of term insurance at the same age. This whole scheme is another ploy by the company to drain your purse into their coffers. Sadly enough, most insurance agents neglect to fully explain this option to you.

"But when insurance companies receive a policy which even they can't afford to fully insure themselves, what do they do? They buy 'reinsurance' from other companies, and so share the risk among many companies. This is perfectly legitimate, as there are few companies that can risk insuring a million- or multimillion-dollar policy; but what type of 'reinsurance' do they buy? Do they buy cash-value insurance from each other, which they assure the public is far superior? No! They do not! Insurance companies *always* buy term insurance when they buy from each other. Yet they discourage the public from buying term insurance."

"Holmes, this is scandalous. Can we not put an end to this? Is this practice not illegal?"

"No, Watson, there is no simple way of ending this practice. Because these companies are the wealthiest in the country, they are powerful. Many of their executives dabble in politics. Since almost all the public ever hears about life insurance is from one of the captive agents of these very companies, you can imagine how widespread is the ignorance concerning the workings of these companies. The few people who try to honestly inform the public what they are buying are voices crying out in the wilderness, lacking the money or platform to make their side of the story widely known.

"Moreover, the government would hardly dare to attack the business these companies do, because the taxes the companies pay and the government bonds they buy, which help finance the national debt, have linked them inextricably with the government, and the government covets their tax dollars—a very cozy arrangement which the government won't abandon unless they are shamed out of it by public outcry. Those taxes the insurance companies pay to the state government, by the way, come out of your pocket, Watson. About five percent of the cost of the policy is marked for state premium taxes, another fact which too few people know.

"The attitudes of the victims play into this matter also. You know yourself that people hesitate to consider their approaching death, so they usually don't inform themselves and 'shop around' to see what financial arrangements can be made. No, they sit contentedly hoping that Death will spare them, of all people, until a 'friendly' insurance agent comes along and persuades them to buy a whole-life policy; when that happens, they don't have the knowledge to resist his false arguments and persuasive sales pitch.

"The agent, Watson, is as relentless as a leech once he decides you need to be insured by him. The training I've been receiving as an agent is completely oriented toward making me a company salesman; almost none of it has been directed toward serving the true financial needs of my client. Unless, of course, you assume that the financial interest of the client is exactly what will maximize the profit of the insurance company and its agents. The Trupolitan Company assumes this is the case, and they train their agents on this principle.

"I was confined to a London hotel room with a workbook to memorize. Yonder lies its ashes. I may not have memorized it to the satisfaction of my general or managing agent, but I saw enough of it to learn the attitudes of the company, and how they infect their agents with their values.

"My training began with a full day of work on 'How to Get into the House.' Gems of knowledge are transmitted such as 'Get rid of cigarettes and gum, walk briskly, use the pavement, knock, ring or buzz authoritatively, and assume you will get in.' You see, Watson, the Trupolitan Company not only takes nothing for granted in the matter of their prospective agents being totally devoid of manners and salesmanship, but also begins to persuade them that they are doing the client a much-needed service. Their goal at this point is simply to get into the house. All statements end with the magic words 'May I come in?' "

"This pleading for admittance by the agent reminds me of a sensational novel I've read, Holmes," I said. "I had a fascinating conversation with a young author named Bram Stoker at the Lyceum Theater, where he works. In his book *Dracula,* he stresses the point that the vampire must induce his victims to come to him willingly. I particularly remember an episode in which he uses the words 'Enter freely, and of your own will.' Evidently evil must be invited in order to get a foothold."

"That's a very appropriate parallel, Watson. I see your literary associates are giving you a fine liberal education. Yes, the agent is powerless unless invited into the client's home, and perhaps calling the client his 'victim' would be more accurate, and to the point.

"Once inside the house, I was to glance around the home, to 'case the joint,' as my criminal associates would put it. I was to discuss the family's financial situation, their plans for the future or lack of them, the health and age of the breadwinner, the shattering effects the family would suffer if 'something happened.' Grotesque visual aids drive this point home: pictures of a family without the father present, or of a widow grieving in a cemetery. They call this tactic 'driving the hearse up to the front door.' It is guaranteed to make the client uncomfortable.

"We memorized a script containing all possible objections to buying life insurance, with convenient answers for sidestepping the objections. Redefining words, turning phrases around, and appealing to fear or greed in the client are all common and profitable techniques for selling insurance. This Abernathy who came to us had barely begun to pull tricks out of his bag of techniques before his presentation broke down.

"His next move would have been according to a four-stage plan that agents parrot to clients. The first step is to 'build up the problem to disturb the client.' Driving the hearse up to the door, you see. Next he plays upon greed by promising that the whole-life insurance policy virtually pays for itself in the long run, so your insurance 'costs you nothing.' That is a phrase that agents relish. They also continue to make morbid references to keep the client disturbed and uncomfortable.

"The agent then proceeds to 'consider possible solutions,' as the workbook puts it. Of course, the script is written so that all objections are turned aside and the whole-life insurance policy emerges

"Agents describe the shattering effects a family would suffer if 'something' should happen . . . evoke pictures of a widow grieving in a cemetery. . . . This tactic is called 'driving the hearse up to the front door.'"

as the heaven-sent solution to financial insecurity. The last stage is to close the sale—get the client to 'buy now. Tomorrow may be too late.'

"One of the finest revelations my instructor gave to me was 'The buying public is not sophisticated.' This was driven home with an analogy which they felt would give us, the agent, the right mental attitude to close the sale: 'The Arena Metaphor.'

"In this scenario, the approach of the agent to the client's door represents the parade at the start of a bullfight. You enter proud, erect, self-assured. Need I tell you who represents the bull? The hapless client, of course. What more appropriate symbol for the 'unsophisticated' public could the Trupolitan Company choose than a raging, stupid bullock?"

"Holmes, this is obscene! You mean that blatherskite Abernathy considered me a bull, and himself the matador?"

"Very perceptive, Watson; you're racing ahead of me. The toreador is represented by the charts and graphs that soften up, confuse, and weaken the client, just as the harassment by the real toreador and the sharp lance of the picador weaken the bull. Then the masterful matador Abernathy makes his entrance, confusing you with passes and veronicas of his cape—excuse me, I mean his presentation—until you are ready for the 'kill.' The 'kill' is the agent's term for closing the sale. This analogy makes the process much more romantic, and also puts the agent into the proper frame of mind to pursue you to the 'kill'—pardon, I mean closing the sale. It's just a pity that clients don't gore their insurance agents occasionally."

"Are there no laws prohibiting these tactics?" I asked.

"Not now, Watson, and not ever if the insurance companies have their way. Quite frequently, a public-spirited legislator or lobbyist will come along and propose a 'truth-in-life-insurance' law which would require the agent to tell the customer how much of his premium goes into the death benefit, how much makes up the cash values, how much he earns on it, how much insurance protection he is receiving after his cash values are subtracted from the death benefit, and how much commission the agent receives on the sale. The companies, however, often have former agents and executives sitting in the government hearing rooms and legislative chambers just waiting to quash any such suggestion; reform is often proposed, but rarely passed. Even the state insurance commissioners, who are supposed to regulate and supervise the practices of insurance companies are, themselves, often mere political appointees or elected puppets who are putty in the hands of the insurance companies and their agents."

"Is there then no way of breaking this vicious circle? Can't this horrendous fraud be brought to an end?"

"There is, Watson, and you can play a part in it. Public education is the key to success. When the public knows of these deceptive practices, they will demand laws against them, and when the public is aroused, no legislator will dare hold up the much-needed reform of the insurance industry. When that happens, we will be free of the scourge of these phony cash values and dividends, and the companies will be forced to compete on an honorable basis. Indeed, the insurance companies will gain a new reputation for themselves as the true benefactors of the public after that day, instead of their present appearance of smiling into your face while picking your pocket behind your back. Watson, are you willing to do your small part to bring about that day?"

"I most certainly am, Holmes."

"Then write up this little adventure of ours, publish it, and all your readers will be forewarned against the deceptive tricks of any insurance agents who might come knocking at their door. We can only hope that then people will be sufficiently aroused to demand that their legislators put an end to these deceptive practices; at least we will have thrown our influence on the side of the working people, who suffer the most grievously from the tactics of these unscrupulous companies.

"Now, then, Watson, I suggest you take pen in hand while these events are still fresh in our minds. I shall play a few divertimentos on my violin while you make your notes, and in the morning I shall don my insurance agent costume one last time. I shall make one last trek to the home office of Trupolitan and shall resign 'owing to the difficulties of making further sales,' just as eighty or ninety percent of all agents do after they've sold policies to their friends and

Holmes solved the conspiracy, and left it to me to expose the tactics of these unscrupulous companies that deceive the people.

family. Indeed, I'll probably be just in time to join young Abernathy's farewell party, for he also has announced his plans to leave the office. I'll leave you to your paper and pen, Watson, with my heartiest thanks for introducing me to this entirely novel form of crime and conspiracy, which is immune to attack by the police, since it is perfectly legal; let's hope that will soon be corrected."

And with that, Holmes lowered himself into his overstuffed chair and began to produce lovely and haunting melodies from his Stradivarius violin, while I took to my desk and began to set this incredible tale to paper.

3

'Points to Remember

Incredible as it may seem, all the tricks Holmes described are being perpetrated today. Just to review them in order:

(1) The whole point of buying life insurance is to provide financial security in case of unexpected death; yet the typical insurance agent usually persuades his client to buy a cash-value type of life policy which pays much, much smaller death benefits than a term insurance policy costing the same.

(2) The cash-value policy doesn't pay a large enough death benefit to be worthwhile. It may pay the costs of burial, but what will the family live on after that? A term policy will provide long-term income at a lower price.

(3) On the other hand, the "cash-surrender values" of the whole-life policy don't earn enough to even overcome inflation. As one of the top insurance salesmen in the country, Northwestern Mutual's David Hilton, admitted in the April 12, 1976 *Wall Street Journal,* "There are potentially better investments." In fact, almost any investment is better than a whole-life insurance policy. Because the rate of interest it pays is so low and doesn't keep up with the rate of inflation, you actually lose money in the long run. A U.S. Senate Subcommittee survey of the best selling dividend-paying cash-value life policies from 198 companies found that they had an average rate of return of 3½ percent after 20 years. And the average rate of interest on non-dividend-paying policies was a meager 2¼ percent.

(For the further devastating effect of inflation on both the policy-holder and whole-life insurance companies, see Appendix A: Excerpts from the *Trend Report*, page 135.)

(4) If you examine the fine print in your whole-life insurance policy, you'll find a clause informing you that the company can make you wait up to six months before you may receive your cash values.

(5) If you die while insured by a whole-life policy, those cash values disappear. The company will pay your beneficiary only the face amount of the policy; no extra cash values will be awarded.

(6) The insurance agent is paid far more commission dollars from his company for selling whole-life insurance than the cheaper term policies. This fact obviously interferes with the professional judgment of the agent, who is tempted to line his own pocket by selling as much whole-life insurance as possible.

There is a crying need for a just way of compensating brokers and agents for selling term insurance products. For one thing, a head of household looking for insurance should go to an independent agent or broker, rather than a "captive" one. (The "captive agent" is one who works for a specific company and must ally him- or herself with the company's most lucrative product.) Then, perhaps, depending on whether the agent is simply selling you protection or setting up an entire financial planning program, which many agents are qualified to do, he or she could be paid an hourly fee by the client or a percentage of the family's annual income—whichever is fairer.

(7) Your whole-life insurance agent may promise you all sorts of continuing services when he sells you your policy, but he won't tell you that the average agent lasts only six months in the business. Most agents drop out of the profession after they've signed up their family, friends, and college pals for policies, and they've run out of acquaintances to impose on. You'll probably have to deal with a different agent in the future, which will affect the service you'll receive.

(8) The "service" you do receive from your whole-life agent is likely to be self-serving, since the training of agents is oriented toward selling ever-increasing amounts of whole-life insurance rather than objectively considering financial alternatives and guiding the client toward maximizing his own profit.

(9) Whole-life insurance is often sold under the name of "paid-up insurance" at a certain age. What happens with these policies, however, is that you pay even higher premiums at younger ages so that the policy can be "paid up" by age 65, 50, or whatever. In a real sense, however, it is never "paid up," because the interest you lose on your cash values, which you must leave with the company to keep the policy "paid up," is a hidden annual cost.

(10) Term insurance is available up to age 100 from some companies that specialize in this particular type of insurance. This makes term insurance as "permanent" as any whole-life policy on the market, which stops being insurance at age 100 because your cash values at that time equal the death benefit, and you are completely self-insured.

(11) Whole-life insurance is often pushed on young people, sometimes when there is obviously no need for insurance, because it is supposedly cheaper at younger ages. A moment's reflection will show you that while the annual premium may be lower at a younger age, you are paying over a longer period of time and losing the use of your money (and interest) over a longer period of time, so ultimately the cost of the policy isn't really any lower.

One of the worst abuses of the life insurance industry, by the way, is a policy frequently called "college life," whereby college kids—who need life insurance like a hole in the head to begin with —are regularly inveigled into signing up for whole-life policies. Since college kids don't often have much money of their own, they pay for the first annual premiums by promissory notes. And when those notes "mature" or fall due, the kid has to pay—whatever his current thoughts on the subject. Again, "college life" is simply a symptom of the entire problem—most especially consumer ignorance when it comes to term versus whole-life insurance. (For more about the specific "college life" problem, try to get hold of a copy of *The Shopper's Guide to Life Insurance for College Students —What the Agents Don't Tell You*, by Joel W. Makower and Arthur E. Rowse.)

(12) The average length of time that any life insurance policy is kept in force is about seven to nine years. Most people let them lapse during this period. In the case of whole-life or cash-value

policies, you are grossly overpaying in the early years—a time when term insurance is relatively inexpensive. So even if the individual didn't let the policy lapse (if you do, you get next to nothing back), a 30-year-old man or woman would overpay for about 27 years until the cost of the premiums on term insurance (which increase at a much later age) would approach the cost of cash-value insurance. The effect is, in any event, that you have been sold some *very* expensive term insurance, something that would have cost a lot less, if you had started with term to begin with.

(13) The mutual insurance companies, the giants of the industry, add to this an extra overcharge on the policy. This overcharge raises the cost of the average policy as much as 30 percent. You could take this same money and invest it yourself and get a far better return than the insurance company which may pay you as a so-called "dividend." And remember, you may not receive the full overcharge back as a "dividend," nor are the "dividends" guaranteed!

(14) The industry's successful emphasis on selling cash-value life insurance has enabled its companies to amass assets now totaling over a third of a trillion dollars. In 1976, insurance companies took in $18 billion that came not from the sales of insurance, but from the investment of their monumental assets.

(15) The overwhelming financial power of the life insurance companies has allowed them to misinform the public through misleading commercials and advertisements, and has given them unfair lobbying power over Congress and the state legislatures. Today, the life insurance industry is the largest virtually unregulated business in America. It has absolutely no federal standards to meet, and most states have left the life insurance companies pretty much alone.

(16) Remember to review your economic needs along with your insurance program, and be sure to *commit* yourself to an appropriate term insurance *and* a separate investment/savings program that suits your needs.

There are two ways to put an end to the disgraceful practices that exist in the life insurance industry and guarantee consumers proper protection. The first way is to examine your own insurance policy, if you have one, and see whether you've been sold a cash-value policy. Chances are that's what you've got, since 75 percent of the life insurance written in America is cash-value. We will explain how to cancel that policy and what to look for in a new insurance agent and a new policy, if necessary.

The other approach is collective; there must be federal standards to guarantee "truth in life insurance" to the consumer. It won't be easy, since the insurance companies have successfully fought off regulation and reform for 125 years. However, if numerous people, including you, demand laws to protect the insurance buyer, Congress will respond. The only thing a Congressman fears more than an angry special-interest group is an aroused public. Your voice will help!

4

The Policies: What Type of Term Insurance to Buy

As consumers have been catching on to the trick of cash values and "dividends," they've been demanding more and better term insurance. Some companies responded to that demand by offering a whole spectrum of term insurance policies, ranging in quality from excellent to less than satisfactory.

Annual Renewable Level Term

As the name implies, you have the right to renew the policy annually at guaranteed rates without having to show evidence of insurability—via medical exams, for example. Renewal is automatic each year regardless of any change in your health. The death benefit remains level throughout the lifetime of the policy, with an increasing premium each year according to your age. Despite what whole-life salesmen say about term insurance, there is nothing "temporary" about this type of policy. It can be renewed to age 100. Each year, you evaluate your insurance needs and buy just as much as you think necessary. Of course, if you want to increase your policy and buy more term coverage from the company, you will have to meet the company's medical qualifications. However, most people will buy less term insurance as the years go by simply because their children are growing up and coming closer to the day they leave home and no longer depend on their parents for financial support.

Another benefit you get from this policy is that it allows you to keep pace with inflation. Each year, your dollar is worth a bit less because of inflation; so as time goes by, you are actually paying the insurance company a smaller part of your income with inflated dollars. Of course, you must realize that inflation is also chipping away at the value of the death benefit. However, this is the best way to buy term insurance, because it offers you the maximum amount of protection for the money during the years when it is needed the most.

CHART B

STRAIGHT-LINE DECREASE

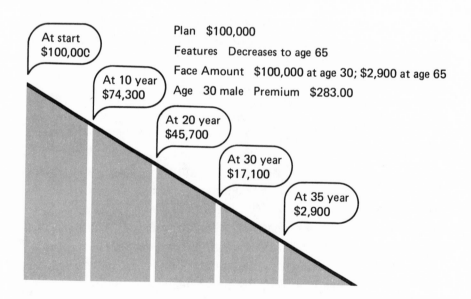

Five-year Renewable and Convertible

You renew the policy every five years instead of annually. The death benefit remains level. Like annual renewable term, you can reduce the amount of the death benefit as you wish.

Decreasing Term to Age 65, 70, or 100

You pay the same amount of money each year, and the amount of the death benefit decreases each year. There are good and bad decreasing term policies; in some the death benefit drops off too rapidly while you are young and need a fairly large amount of protection. Have the agent show you a graph of how the benefits

CHART C

CURVE-LINE DECREASE

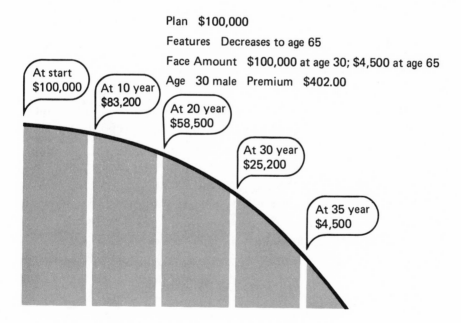

Plan $100,000

Features   Decreases to age 65

Face Amount $100,000 at age 30; $4,500 at age 65

Age 30 male Premium $402.00

At start $100,000

At 10 year $83,200

At 20 year $58,500

At 30 year $25,200

At 35 year $4,500

decline over time. If the benefits fall in a straight line from the upper left to the lower right corner of the graph, the benefits may be falling too quickly for your needs. (See Chart B.) They should fall in a gentle curve, staying high for the first few years and then gradually falling like a thrown ball that travels straight and then curves toward the ground. By age 64, you should still have about 5 percent of the original death benefit left. (See Chart C.)

Level Term Insurance to Age 65 or 70

This is very, very expensive. As you get older, your risk of dying increases, so your insurance costs more in advance. This policy will pay you the same high death benefit during the time you own it. Most people don't need this type of protection; it's far wiser to get a decreasing term policy or annual renewable term and invest elsewhere the difference in premium costs, so when you do grow old your investments will provide the financial stability your family might need without you.

Deposit Term Insurance

Sometimes called deposit annual renewable term (DART) or modified-premium whole-life insurance, this is neither true term insurance nor is it exactly whole-life. When you buy term policies like these—usually for a ten-year term—you pay a deposit the first year (ranging from $3 to $10 per $1000 of insurance) in addition to the premium. The insurance company invests the deposit and, at the end of the ten years, pays you back your deposit with interest. If they pay 7.2 percent interest, for example, your money will almost double in ten years, and the interest income is tax-deferred.

The growth of the deposit is designed to lower the cost of the policy over a period of ten years by encouraging you to keep the policy in force, since dropping or lapsing policies early generally increases insurance rates. In theory, deposit term should be a good buy because companies can significantly reduce the costs associated with dropped policies in setting their term rates. However, too many companies pass these savings along to agents and brokers in commissions instead of passing them along to policyholders. In fact, we have not been able to find any deposit term policies that are lower in cost than regular annual renewable term policies without any additional first-year deposits. Nevertheless, deposit annual renewable term insurance, combined with a low-load (low or no upfront administrative charges) flexible premium annuity (a savings plan; see Chapter 9, Investing Your Savings), can be financially attractive, *particularly* when this combination plan is compared with a cream-of-the-crop whole-life policy.

Before you buy any deposit term policy, ask yourself:

(1) Do I need or want level death protection for ten full years? In short, should I commit myself to one policy for ten years?

(2) Could I use the deposit money for other investments that might pay a tax-deferred 7.2 percent *annually* rather than at the end of ten years?

(3) Am I willing to lose part or all of the deposit if I have to drop the policy before ten years elapse? (A number of these policies do pay some cash values by the fifth year.)

(4) Does the company guarantee me term insurance up to age 100, or must I convert to whole-life at age 65?

(5) Is the "cost" really going to be lower for the full ten years than a non-deposit, annual renewable term policy over the same period of years? Have your independent broker or agent compare the "costs" of deposit term policies with low-cost, non-deposit, annual renewable term policies. If you do decide on a deposit term policy, shop around to find the least expensive one. Some are better than others.

The term policy you select should allow you to switch from one kind of term policy to another without taking another physical examination. Some companies will only allow you to convert term to whole-life insurance. Your term insurance should also be guaranteed renewable without a physical exam, and it should be inexpensive. Compare prices on identical policies offered by different companies. When you call the company, tell the agent you are shopping, comparing prices, and ask for the lowest rates.

Some companies use your age on your last birthday instead of your nearest birthday, which might be coming up. A low-cost age-last-birthday policy is very competitive. Don't look merely at the first year's premium for any term policy. Make certain you compare renewal rates, for instance, every five years or so until your late fifties and early sixties. Increasing premiums are found in annual renewable term, in deposit term, and in five-year renewable and convertible term policies.

Some companies' policies are more competitive at younger ages than middle or older ages; other companies are the opposite. Many companies have very good prices on large policies, those with death benefits in excess of $100,000. Some companies offer excellent buys at even higher levels of death benefits.

Most companies charge a policy fee, usually $10 to $25 annually. A good independent broker or agent can help you with your price comparisons and steer you through the maze.

When shopping for your term insurance, do make absolutely sure that it's term you're getting. Beware of any gimmicks that becloud the fact that a policy may actually be whole-life—sometimes masquerading as something else.

Option to Revert

Some companies are offering annual renewable term policies containing an option to revert back to lower rates after medically requalifying at five-year intervals. These policies are worth considering, particularly if you are in the very best of health. But there is a danger in buying one of these policies. If you should become medically impaired and cannot qualify for the lower rates, you will face much higher rates than if you had originally purchased a guaranteed low-cost annual renewable level term policy *without* an option to revert.

Variable Life

Variable life insurance is another new wrinkle that a handful of companies are trying out. In addition to the usual whole-life policy, you pay extra into a variable-separate account. The money in this extra account is then invested in the stock market and managed by the insurance company. Your beneficiary can never receive a smaller death benefit than is specified on the face of the policy, and will receive the funds in the variable account besides. The value of the variable account may increase or decrease, depending on the progress of the stock market and the wisdom of the insurance company financial managers.

Adjustable Life Insurance

Adjustable life insurance is another new wrinkle, but actually it is nothing but whole-life insurance in sheep's clothing. Agents are touting adjustable life as an answer to the problems of cash-value insurance, but the features of adjustable life are disturbingly familiar. It has "dividends," it is "paid-up," it is flexible to match increasing cost of living. But, unfortunately, when you look at how much this policy costs per $1000 of coverage at any particular age, you find that it doesn't begin to compare with a low-cost term policy and a separate savings and investment program. Adjustable life insurance is just one more attractively packaged pitfall to be avoided.

A new tool that some agents are now using, and which you should look at with great caution, is analysis of different policies by computer. The thing to remember about computers is that they can only give answers that are as good as the information that's fed into them. Some companies only program their computers to compare a few policies; others compare a wide range of policies from many companies, which gives a much more unbiased picture of how good a policy is and helps you decide what your true needs are. Ask the agent how many policies the computer is programmed to analyze. If the computer tells you that whole-life is a better buy than term, it is likely that an overly expensive term policy has been compared with a whole-life policy.

There are ways of buying term insurance without any agent at all, and some of the following methods are worth looking into:

Group Life Insurance

Group life insurance rates are calculated by averaging the ages of all the employees, so if you are a middle-aged or elderly man in a company of young workers, you can get a very low rate. If, on the other hand, all your fellow workers are older than you, you will pay more than if you bought individual life insurance. The only way to avoid making a mistake is to compare the group rate with the rate you could get if you bought your own individual policy. Of course, if your employer is footing the bill, take all group insurance for which you are eligible.

Section 79 of the Internal Revenue Code allows corporations to purchase individual term-life policies under a master contract for selected employees and make the premiums deductable as a corporate expense. An extension of Section 79 is *retired lives reserve*, which provides group life benefits *after* retirement. This is accomplished by the corporation paying the premiums *before* retirement and at the same time taking the tax deduction.

Credit Life

Credit life is a small term insurance policy that is issued through a lending institution, the idea being that if you die before repaying your loan your creditor can recover the debt by being the beneficiary of the policy. Credit life rates vary considerably and can be excessively high, so you might want to consider insuring yourself through your own term company, which might be much less expensive. You are not required by law to take the credit life through the lending institution, and can shop elsewhere for insurance that performs, for all practical purposes, the same function.

Savings Bank Life Insurance

Savings bank life insurance is a plan through which a local bank acts as the insurance agent, selling policies over the counter. So far it is only available to residents and those who work in New York, Connecticut, and Massachusetts—in maximum amounts of $30,000, $10,000, and $41,000, respectively for each state. Numerous cost comparisons have been done of their policies, and their prices are very favorable. If you live in one of these three states, you should definitely consider their term rates.

The Wisconsin State Life Fund

The Wisconsin State Life Fund was established in Wisconsin in 1911 after the Armstrong hearings and Wisconsin's own investigations revealed nationally scandalous improper practices of many life insurance companies. The fund is fascinating in that its existence vividly proves that the commercial insurance industry could deliver inexpensive insurance to the consumer but chooses not to. Like savings bank life insurance, the fund offers a variety of life insurance products. One unique aspect of their "mutual" style policy is that the dividends from the fund are substantial, but the premiums charged are lower than many commercial companies, so you are not being gouged. The fund, administered by the Insurance Commissioner of Wisconsin, is open to residents and non-residents while in the state. Unfortunately, the maximum death benefit that can be purchased is only $10,000; and the big insurance companies and their agents have successfully lobbied to prevent the fund from advertising.

RIDERS

Once you've found the right kind of term insurance for you and your family, it might pay to investigate what kind of *riders* are available with what type of policy. Riders are clauses that sometimes give you extra benefits, for which you are charged an extra fee. Sometimes the benefit is worth the fee—sometimes not.

Waiver of Premium

When you're shopping about for a term policy, check into what sort of waiver-of-premium clause the policy has. What this means is that if you are totally disabled for six months or more, the company will pay the premium for you until you are well enough to resume payments. When you recover, you do not have to pay back the missed premiums. This is a good benefit and it can be quite inexpensive.

It pays to compare waiver-of-premium rates, as some companies that charge low term rates try to recoup by charging fairly high rates for their waiver-of-premium clause. It is also worthwhile to compare the definitions that different companies use to limit their waiver of premium. They can vary substantially over the definition of disability, the waiting period before benefits are payable, the age before which disability must occur, and the maximum time during which premiums will be waived. You can avoid these problems altogether, however, and may do better for yourself by keeping four to six months of savings in a bank *and* signing up for disability income insurance protection. If you do that, then you won't need this extra feature.

Family Benefit Rider

Another feature to consider is the family benefit rider. This provides a small amount of protection on the wife and children in the event of their deaths. It is an inexpensive way to get a small amount of protection for them, and it is far better to get a big term insurance policy with a family rider than to be buying cash-value whole-life policies on each person in the family—or even separate term policies for that matter. With some companies this rider will even guarantee the future insurability of your children.

Accidental Death Benefit

The "accidental death benefit" is a policy rider that agents often persuade people to buy. This rider, often called "double indemnity," is a clause which states that the company will pay extra benefits if your death is accidental. Of course, you pay extra for this rider, too.

Generally you will be better off if you buy enough death protection to satisfy the needs of your beneficiary whether your death is accidental or not. The odds are strongly against accidental death. The *Life Insurance Fact Book '77* notes that among causes of death in 1976, accidents accounted for only 8.6 percent. Of these, 3.1 percent were auto accidents. You knew that the odds were against your dying in the first place. If you do die, the odds are about nine to one against accidental death. Consequently, the "double indemnity" rider probably isn't worth buying.

The best *Double Indemnity* we know is the film by that name, which featured Fred MacMurray, Barbara Stanwyck, and Edward G. Robinson.

Guaranteed Insurability

Guaranteed insurability is a rider which guarantees that you can buy more insurance (usually whole-life only) in the future even if your health changes. This sounds good, but it is better to buy term insurance in a large enough quantity so that you won't need to add to the death protection later. It is cheap enough. If you die tomorrow, what good is a clause that guarantees you the right to buy more insurance years from now? It is much better to be adequately insured with term now than to be underprotected now with a guarantee that you can buy more whole-life insurance later.

There are a few term insurance companies which will automatically increase your premium and your death benefit to keep pace with inflation, as measured in the consumer price index. For example, if inflation were to go up 6 percent next year, your death benefit and premiums would rise by the same amount. Naturally, you pay for this extra feature from the companies that offer it.

Social Security

Social Security is a financial plan which sooner or later affects almost all of us who continually pay money into the program. Sometimes we even get some of it back. Most life insurance is sold in connection with Social Security benefits, the idea being that the benefits will take care of your essential needs and the insurance will give you security.

Social Security is a weak reed to lean on, however, for several reasons. The problem is that you get enough to survive on, but just barely. We know several people who are living on their Social Security payments, and all of them have had to make reductions in their standard of living. In addition, they periodically receive their checks late, or miss them altogether, which throws their finances into a shambles for months until a new check can be reissued. Social Security is a nice program to have behind you if you need it, but it's better to arrange your finances so that you won't need it.

Another reason why Social Security will be unreliable in the future is the way the program is run. When you pay money into the program, that money is not saved or invested for you; it goes right out again to pay benefits for someone who is currently retired or disabled. From the start of the program and through recent years, people were satisfied with the program, because they had put money into it for only part of their working lives, and now are receiving subsistence income. This worked because of the growing population; more people were putting money into the program than were drawing it out.*

Now, however, the population growth of the United States has been stabilized, and the post–World War II "baby boom" is over. When people born in the late 1940s and 1950s want to retire, they will discover that there are more retired people and fewer workers than there are today. Those workers may well balk at the idea of supporting all us old folks in the year 2001, at least at the level that Social Security provides now. There is a good chance that in the future the value of Social Security benefits will decline, so any insurance program that relies on Social Security as a major source of retirement income or protection for one's family is whistling in the dark. Better to play it safe and finance your own retirement.

Late in 1977, Congress authorized hefty increases in Social Security taxes to keep the system financially solvent through the year 2000. However, a Washington *Post* study has suggested that if the economy doesn't keep up with the optimistic predictions that some economists have made, another tax increase in the mid-1980s will be necessary. The benefits will be paid, though, no matter what. A former Commissioner of Social Security, James B. Caldwell, has stated, "The Social Security system is as sound as the United States government." One wonders if it's fair to invert the statement and assert that the government is as sound as the Social Security system.

* Suggested reading: *Social Security . . . Universal or Selective?*—a debate between Milton Friedman and Wilbur Cohen published in 1972 by American Enterprise Institute, 1150 17th St. N.W., Washington, D.C. 20036

In either case, the proclamation doesn't inspire one with the same confidence it might have years ago.

A partial solution to the Social Security problem might be for the government to allow people tax credits for the life insurance premiums they've paid for, and to encourage them to set up their own retirement program. Then, with a practical enough protection and retirement plan, they could get out of Social Security if they wished. The tax credit, for example, would work this way for a family consisting of a husband, wife, and two children aged two and four. This family would need at least 16 years of protection, until the youngest child reached the age of 18. Let's further suppose that the husband takes out a decreasing term policy at age 25, which is good until age 65; that the family income is $14,000; and that the husband thinks his family could live without him on $12,000 a year. This family, then, would need a total of $192,000 in protection, which they could get in a decreasing term insurance policy for $535.68 a year, which is $44.64 monthly, a total of 3¾ percent of the husband's income.

Under the tax credit plan, the husband would be able to deduct the full cost of that $535.68 insurance premium from his Social Security taxes. This is a good deal for the U.S. government, since it cannot provide that kind of protection for only $535.68 a year. If the husband took the $535.68 that he's now deducted on his taxes and put it into a tax-deferred savings account for his retirement, he would have $104,241 to retire on if he could get 7 percent interest on the money for 40 years. This would be in addition to other programs he may now be enrolled in. This may be better than Social Security can do for people in the future.

Social Security, on the other hand, also offers you income if you become disabled and are unable to work. This is a possibility that many people never consider. They buy life insurance, but not "disability income insurance." Social Security will provide for a disabled person, but there are several important restrictions to consider. First, the Social Security system makes the decision as to whether you are truly disabled or not and how much you will receive. You must wait five full months before you can begin collecting disability payments from Social Security. Most importantly, you cannot collect Social Security disability income if you are able to be "gainfully employed," even in some job outside your field, and earn more than $200 a month.

Suppose, for example, you were a highly paid commercial artist who suddenly lost your sight and could no longer draw or paint or do whatever earned you a good salary. You might, if all of your experience is in the art field, be able to get a low-paying job outside the field that didn't require vision. Two hundred dollars a month is very low, and would make you ineligible to collect Social Security. Now the fact is that in time you might want to take a job outside your field, maybe even at low pay. But if it is your special ability that is being insured, plus your capacity to earn an income with it, then you should receive some compensation whatever your future holds—and most especially if it holds a very low income.

One can buy private disability income insurance that overcomes these problems. With private insurance, you have contracted with the company to pay you if you are disabled, and the company doesn't have as much latitude to reject your claim as Social Security does. You can buy disability income insurance that will begin paying benefits as soon as two weeks after you're disabled. However, this is rather expensive, and if you will wait 30, 60, or 90 days before collecting benefits, your premiums will be cheaper. You can contract with the insurance company so that you can still collect your benefits if you work another job, but you do not have to take a job outside your field when you have a private disability income insurance policy.

If you buy a private policy, be sure to get a "non-cancelable" one. Then the company cannot alter the terms of the policy, even if you get sick or change jobs. You should also get coverage for partial or recurrent disability, and avoid the "return-of-premium" type of disability insurance. This is a gimmick for overpricing policies in the same way as is done with whole-life insurance.

As an example of what you can get in a good disability policy: A 30-year-old man could pay about $23 a month for a policy that will pay him $800 a month to age 65 in the case of sickness, or for his lifetime in the case of accident—*if he waits three months before beginning to collect his benefits.* Having such insurance means that you don't need to maintain a large savings account as a cushion in the event of disability. Many businessmen buy this kind of insurance so they can then put their own money into their businesses.

How Much Insurance Do You Need?

Well, with all these different types of policies in mind, we get down to the crux of the matter: How much protection do you need? If you and your wife work and have few financial obligations, very little, perhaps. In any event, when you're considering how much to buy, you should sit down with your financial adviser (an independent agent or broker) and calculate your family's expenses and income needs for each five-year period into the future. (Of course, you won't be considering your own share of the expenses.) Consider taxes, inflation, mortgage payments, educational funds and any other debts. (See Appendix E: Financial Planning Kit, page 163. It's the kind of information an agent or adviser will need to help you.)

Then calculate how much your family will have after estate or other taxes and any other expenses are deducted from your assets if you should die. Don't include risky investments or investments that might be hard to liquidate. Add into the family assets Social Security payments, interest on investments, and any other outside income that they will receive.

Now subtract their guaranteed income from how much they will need. The amount of insurance you will need should cover the difference—the amount your other investments won't provide. Since your assets will (you hope) be increasing and your family's need for income declining as children leave home, by the time you are in your fifties, your need for insurance should be dropping.

Generally, to maintain a good standard of living, if you have one child, you should be thinking in terms of *at least* $100,000 of term insurance; for two children, $150,000; $175,000 for three children, and an extra $25,000 for each additional child.

If you really feel that you can't afford the above, here is another way to calculate your family's *absolute bare minimum income needs.* The table below is based on a family of two adults and two children.

You simply pick your income level, check the percentage figures given for the age of your spouse, and multiply one by the other. For example, a man earning $15,000, with a 25-year-old wife, should insure for $67,500 if he wants his family to try to maintain their standard of living with 75 percent of their former income. If he thinks they can settle for 60 percent of their former income, he can insure for $45,000. This table shows minimal amounts. You may be well advised to add about 25 percent to each amount. The table takes Social Security benefits and an approximately 5 percent inflation rate into account.

These amounts may sound incredibly high, especially compared with the $10,000 or $15,000 whole-life policy most people own. But consider the cost of living today—and tomorrow. Consider that a surviving wife and a one-year-old child need three meals daily. If they can get by on an average cost of $2 per meal, that totals $12 daily. Over the 17 years until the child is out of public school, he and his mother will need $74,256 *just for food alone*—not counting any other expenses. And that's assuming that the cost of a meal doesn't skyrocket past an average of $2 per meal by 1996!

TABLE A

Your Present Gross Earnings	Present Age of Spouse							
	25 Years*		35 Years*		45 Years*		55 Years†	
	75%	60%	75%	60%	75%	60%	75%	60%
$ 7,500	4.0	3.0	5.5	4.0	7.5	5.5	6.5	4.5
9,000	4.0	3.0	5.5	4.0	7.5	5.5	6.5	4.5
15,000	4.5	3.0	6.5	4.5	8.0	6.0	7.0	5.5
23,500	6.5	4.5	8.0	5.5	8.5	6.5	7.5	5.5
30,000	7.5	5.0	8.0	6.0	8.5	6.5	7.0	5.5
40,000	7.5	5.0	8.0	6.0	8.0	6.0	7.0	5.5
65,000	7.5	5.5	7.5	6.0	7.5	6.0	6.5	5.0

* Assuming federal income taxes for a family of four (two children). There are four exemptions and the standard—or 15% itemized—deductions. State and local taxes are disregarded.
† Assuming you have only two exemptions. (Any children are now grown.)

To calculate the amount of life insurance needed for net replacement level, multiply your present gross salary by the number under that level.

If your gross income or spouse's age fall between the figures shown, take an average between the multiples for nearest salaries and ages.

Social Security benefits will be part of both levels: under present laws, benefits end when the children leave home.

If personal liquid assets (savings, predictable inheritance, retirement plan, investment, etc.) equal one year of gross salary or less, use them as part of the fund for the small emergency reserve and final expenses. If they equal *more* than one year, subtract that extra amount from the insurance needed to replace income.

People with no personal assets who can't afford the 75% level might try for at least 60%. The average family would then face some lowering in level of living but wouldn't be financially devastated.

(Source: Citibank of New York)

5
Making the Switch

Don't cancel your whole-life policies immediately. There are three reasons for keeping them temporarily. First, you want to be sure you have some kind of coverage until you are absolutely certain you have your new term insurance in hand. For one thing, almost all life applications and policies stipulate that the policy takes effect *only if delivered while the insured is alive and in good health.* So, even if you've done everything you're supposed to—even paid your first premium in advance—if you die or get very sick before that policy arrives, there is no coverage. Occasionally, such cases have been contested, and the courts have given some relief, but not enough for you to take a chance on. It would also be a grave mistake to cancel your whole-life policy before getting your term policy, only to discover that because of some health problem, you are now uninsurable.

Secondly, your new policy, as well as your old one, will have a clause in it called the "incontestability clause," which means that the company can nullify the policy if you lied on your application for the new policy. The major reasons that companies nullify policies are for lying about a pre-existing medical condition, or committing suicide during the first two years of the policy. If you don't intend to lie or commit suicide, you should have no worries about switching policies.

Finally, if you wait until the annual renewal date to cancel your whole-life policy, you will get the full cash values due then. If your policy is from a mutual company, you will also get that year's refund ("dividend"). However, even if you wait until that date, the cash values or dividend payment usually will not equal the premiums you paid in. To get your money, send the company a letter like the following:

(Date)

(Your Insurance Company)
(Home Office Address)

> Policy number ——————
> Dated ———————————
> Amount of policy —————
> Name of the insured ———
>
> ——————————————————

Dear Sirs:

Please send me all available cash values plus any dividends and accrued interest on my policy, the number of which appears above. Mail the check to me, at my home address below, as soon as possible. Your immediate attention to this matter will be appreciated as I will need this money within the next two weeks. If there are any forms for me to sign, please send them with the check.

> Thank you,
>
> (Signature of policyowner)
>
> (Address of policyowner)

To sum it up: Don't cancel your old policy until you are safely insured by your new policy.

Your first step is to locate an efficient and knowledgeable insurance agent or broker who represents good companies. If you have a friend who has already converted his whole-life policies to term, ask the name of his agent and seek him out to see if he suits your needs. If you must search out an agent, don't call up just any insurance company and have them send over one of their "captive agents"; look for an independent agent or broker who is able to compare the policies of various companies and find you the best.

Especially avoid the department-store and shopping-center insurance counters. The agents there are associated with only one company, they have even less training than average (which is little enough), and the price of their term products is not competitive. Nor do they run to age 100, which means that at age 65 or 70 you must convert to whole-life or the policy ends.

Also, generally avoid religious and fraternal insurance companies. If you want to give to the church, do it directly and get a tax deduction. Don't think you are helping the church by paying overcharges on an insurance policy. If you do prefer to buy from a fraternal company, bear two things in mind: Many of these companies have an "assessment clause," which states that if they are in financial trouble, they can assess you to get out of debt. If you don't pay the assessment, an interest charge will be added to it. Secondly, fraternal companies have been known to sell people whole-life insurance to cover a mortgage on a home or to cover a loan, when insurance sold for such purposes should *always* be inexpensive term insurance.

Our research has turned up a number of very reliable companies that specialize in selling term insurance. Their financial ratings indicate that they are strong and well managed, and they pay brokers and agents who sell term insurance enough to support themselves. Inclusion in the following list is not an unqualified endorsement for these companies, however, for many also sell whole-life policies to customers who request them. Neither the list or the tables following it are all-inclusive, but they will serve as a starting point for shopping or consulting with your independent agent or broker. Consider the rates of these companies' policies as a constantly changing yardstick for comparing their prices and those of other companies.

The companies are listed alphabetically and are given Best's policyholder Financial Ratings. You can find out more about Best's and how they rate companies at the end of this listing.

American Agency Life Insurance Co.
Box 7430
Atlanta, Georgia 30357
(B+ very good)

Anchor National Life Insurance Co.
Camelback at 22nd St.
Phoenix, Arizona 85016
(A+ excellent)

Crown Life Insurance Co.
120 Bloor St. East
Toronto, Ontario, Canada
   M4W 1B8
(A+ excellent)

Executive Life Insurance Co.
9777 Wilshire Blvd.
Beverly Hills, California 90212
(A+ excellent)

Fireman's Fund—American Life
   Insurance Co.
1600 Los Gamos Drive
San Rafael, California 94911
(A+ excellent)

First Colony Life Insurance Co.
Box 1280
Lynchburg, Virginia 24505
(A+ excellent)

International Life Insurance Co. of
   Buffalo
120 Delaware Ave.
Buffalo, New York 14202
(B+ very good)

Life Insurance Company of Cali-
   fornia
P.O. Box 2700
La Jolla, California 92038
(A excellent)

Life Insurance Co. of New Hamp-
   shire
P.O. Box 2226
Wilmington, Delaware 19899
(A excellent)

North American Co. for Life and
   Health
P.O. Box 466
Chicago, Illinois 60690
(A+ excellent)

North American Life and Casualty
P.O. Box 20
Minneapolis, Minnesota 55440
(A+ excellent)

Northwestern National Life Insurance Company
20 Washington N.E. South
Minneapolis, Minnesota 55401
(A+ excellent)

Occidental Life Insurance Co. of
   California
P.O. Box 2101
Terminal Annex
Los Angeles, California 90051
(A+ excellent)

Old Line Life Insurance Co.
707 N. 11th St.
Milwaukee, Wisconsin 53233
(A+ excellent)

Philadelphia Life Insurance Co.
111 North Broad St.
Philadelphia, Pennsylvania 19107
(A+ excellent)

Presidential Life Insurance Co.
69 Lydecker St.
Nyack, N.Y. 10960
(A excellent)

Security-Connecticut Life Insur-
   ance Co.
Security Dr.
Avon, Connecticut 06001
(A excellent)

Shenandoah Life Insurance Co.
2301 Brambleton Ave. S.W.
Roanoke, Virginia 24015
(A+ excellent)

Teachers Insurance and Annuity
Association
730 Third Ave.
New York, N.Y. 10017
(A+ excellent)

Western National Life Insurance
Co.
205 East 10th St.
Amarillo, Texas 79101
(A excellent)

United Investors Life Insurance Co.
One Crown Center
P.O. Box 1441
Kansas City, Missouri 64141
(A+ excellent)

Zurich-American Life Insurance Co.
111 W. Jackson Blvd.
Chicago, Illinois 60604
(B+ very good)

Best's ratings are based on an analysis of the financial condition and operating performance of an insurance company. The ratings are classified in five gradations A+ and A (excellent); B+ (very good); B (good); C+ (fairly good); C (fair)—and reflect the relative financial strength of the company in comparison to the life/ health insurance industry performance in such vital areas as

(1) Competent underwriting
(2) Control of expenses
(3) Adequate reserves
(4) Sound investments.

Best's ratings are not a recommendation of the specific policy provisions, rates, or claims practices of the insurance company.

The information provided is an accurate digest of the complete reports on the companies which can be found in the 1978 edition of *Best's Insurance Reports.* This publication is compiled independently and without remuneration to the A. M. Best Company, Oldwick, New Jersey 08858.

You may be curious to know how much you should reasonably expect to pay for annual renewable (level) term insurance. The following tables show what you should expect to pay for different amounts of death protection. Generally, the more you buy, the lower the rates. (The tables exclude the Teachers Insurance and Annuity Association, whose very low priced five-year renewable and convertible term policy is limited to employees of colleges, universities, and certain other non-profit educational institutions.)

These prices are for men and include any policy fees that the company might charge, but they *do not* include "waiver of premium" or any other riders. Women can get an advantage called an "age setback." Because women generally live longer than men, their ages are "set" or put back by about three years. Women's rates, using a three-year setback, will be approximately 4 to 10 percent less up to age 35, and graduate as much as 21 percent through age 40. At age 45, rates can be as much as 15 to 24 percent less to age 65. Some really low priced polices, offering a five-year or more setback for women, will result in even greater savings.

(We found three companies that offer annual renewable, convertible, and *revertible* term policies, but we did not include them in the $100,000 and $300,000 price guidelines, because every fifth year the policy *reverts* to an even lower rate—*if you qualify medically*. Otherwise, their prices become substantially higher. We have

TABLE B
RANGE OF ANNUAL PREMIUMS ON $50,000 POLICY

Age	
25	$109 to $150
30	$114 to $150
35	$125 to $161
40	$152 to $211
45	$213 to $296
50	$321 to $453
55	$483 to $696
60	$742 to $1118
65	$1192 to $1763

TABLE C
RANGE OF ANNUAL PREMIUMS ON $100,000 POLICY

Age	
25	$191 to $205
30	$197 to $223
35	$212 to $232
40	$281 to $315
45	$414 to $462
50	$645 to $701
55	$1006 to $1079
60	$1587 to $1681
65	$2488 to $2637

RANGE OF ANNUAL PREMIUMS ON $300,000 POLICY

Age	
25	$533 to $552
30	$560 to $603
35	$586 to $633
40	$769 to $867
45	$1159 to $1299
50	$1837 to $2007
55	$2917 to $3120
60	$4657 to $4971
65	$7336 to $7782

also completely excluded the non-smoker's policy offered by American Agency Life and Executive Life, even though it has lower rates than shown in the guidelines, because none of the other companies we found offered special rates to non-smokers.)

The companies listed above have historically offered low-cost term insurance to the public. Once you've decided how much term insurance you need, you can write or call these companies or an independent broker or agent. Remember, this is *not* a complete list. Other companies are lowering their rates to keep up with the competition.

It may surprise you that most of these companies are not "household names," but the fact is that many smaller insurance companies are actually as strong and managed better than companies that invest in TV commercials. The Hart hearings on the life insurance industry (See Appendix C: Excerpts from the *Hart Hearings*, page 148) confirmed that the huge companies are only about average as to the price of their policies and the efficiency of their management.

If you already own term insurance, you might want to check the rates other companies offer with the rates we show. It may be well worth your time to shop and compare.

When you contact companies, tell them you're interested in term insurance and term insurance only; they'll be happy to have their representative contact you.

When the agent arrives, however, keep your own individual needs in mind. Don't let him persuade you to buy any type of cash-value policy. Also, if you choose decreasing term insurance be sure to get a sample copy of the insurance contract, with a table showing how quickly the death benefits decline year by year.

Make sure if you choose an annual renewable term policy that it allows you to convert the policy to any available term policy of the company, and ideally, allow you to reduce the face amount as you get older.

The next step is filling out the forms for the new policy. Answer all questions truthfully. A false answer could cause the new company to nullify your insurance under the incontestability clause if they discover you lied.

The medical exam is your next hurdle. Don't volunteer medical information to the doctor. Just answer his questions. Also, take the physical in the morning after a good night's sleep and avoid coffee and other stimulants so you are in best shape. Above all, don't try to lie to the doctor; the Medical Information Bureau keeps complete files on people's medical records, so you would probably be caught.

Here is a set of medical questions typical of those asked by the insurance companies:

So far as you know and believe are you in good health and free from impairment?

Have you ever had:

(a) Tuberculosis, asthma, blood spitting, disease of lungs or respiratory system?

(b) High blood pressure, chest pain, heart murmur or disease of heart or circulatory system?

(c) Jaundice, indigestion, ulcer, disease or disorder of stomach, intestines, rectum, liver or gall bladder?

(d) Fainting spells, epilepsy, nervousness, severe headaches, mental disorder or any disease of brain or nervous system?

(e) Albumin, blood or sugar in urine, disease of kidney, bladder, prostate or urinary system?

(f) Rheumatic fever, arthritis, rheumatism, disease of muscles, bones or joints?

(g) Diabetes, goiter, gout?

(h) Cancer, tumor, syphilis?

(i) Defect of sight or hearing, deformity, amputation or paralysis?

(j) Ever been discharged for physical reasons from armed services, or been given a deferred draft classification for physical reasons?

(k) Ever used alcoholic beverages to excess or used drugs or been advised to take treatment for alcoholism or drug habit?

(l) Within five years lived or been closely associated with any person suffering from tuberculosis?

(m) Ever been advised to have a surgical operation, consulted a physician, or been hospitalized during the past 10 years?

A number of insurance companies are much more liberal than others about health requirements. If you have been declined term insurance by a company (or it refuses to write you at standard rates) because of a medical impairment, consult with your independent broker or agent. Ask him to get you term insurance proposals from companies with a liberal underwriting and rating approach. By shopping around, he should find you the lowest-rated policy, and he may even come up with a company willing to write you on a standard non-surcharged basis.

We find that the following companies specialize in writing competitive term insurance even for those people with serious medical disorders, though an extra charge may be made. This list, of course, is not complete. Some of these companies will be more competitive than others, and your broker or agent may know of still other competitive companies.

American Agency Life Insurance Co.
Box 7430
Atlanta, Georgia 30357
(B+ very good)

Executive Life Insurance Co.
9777 Wilshire Blvd.
Beverly Hills, California 90212
(A+ excellent)

First Colony Life Insurance Co.
Box 1280
Lynchburg, Virginia 24505
(A+ excellent)

Guardsman Life Insurance Co.
1025 Ashworth Rd.
West Des Moines, Iowa 50265
(A+ excellent)

Manufacturer's Life Insurance Co.
200 Bloor St. East
Toronto, Ontario, Canada
   M4W 1E5
(A+ excellent)

National Fidelity Life Insurance Co.
1002 Walnut St.
Kansas City, Missouri 64106
(A+ excellent)

New Jersey Life Insurance Co.
Park 80 Plaza West
Saddle Brook, N.J. 07662
(B+ very good)

Presidential Life Insurance Co.
69 Lydecker St.
Nyack, N.Y. 10960
(A excellent)

Security-Connecticut Life Insurance Co.
Security Dr.
Avon, Connecticut 06001
(A excellent)

Standard Security Life Insurance Co. of New York
485 Madison Ave.
New York, N.Y. 10022
(B+ very good)

United Presidential Life Insurance Co.
217 Southcay Blvd. East
Kokomo, Indiana 46901
(A excellent)

When the agent calls back to tell you your policy has been approved, go over it with him to see how long the company is able to challenge your policy under the incontestability clause so you know whether you should keep your whole-life policies for another year or two. Also, ask to have all benefit riders explained to you.

The least expensive way to pay your premiums is annually, because you avoid extra billing charges, which can range from 4.9 to 34.8 percent for semi-annual payment. Some companies will let you pay on a monthly basis without an extra billing charge by using their preauthorized checking system. This allows a draft to be drawn against your checking or savings account on the premium-due date each month.

6
Tallying the Price

If you discover that you own a whole-life policy, don't feel too bad about it. You are in good company. Millions of whole-life policies are currently in the hands of uninformed insurance consumers in America who innocently made the same mistake you did. What you want to do now is calculate just how much you're losing, so you won't regret converting from whole-life to term insurance.

First, get out all your policies and total up how much the death benefit would be if you were to die today. Do not include accidental death or double-indemnity riders.

Second, add up the cash-surrender values of your policies.

Third, subtract the total of the cash-surrender values from the total of the death benefits. The result will tell you how much insurance you are really getting. As Holmes showed Watson, you are insuring yourself for the balance of the protection, since your survivors will only receive the death benefit, not the death benefit plus the cash-surrender values.

Fourth, if you have borrowed money from your insurance policy, find out how much the company is charging you in interest annually. The interest rate can be found written into the fine print on your policy. Multiply that interest rate by the amount of money you still "owe" the company. If you've never borrowed on your policy, ignore this step. If you have borrowed, be sure to add the interest charge to the final cost of your insurance after the last step.

Fifth, multiply the total of the cash-surrender values by 5½ percent. If you weren't giving the insurance company this money, you could expect to earn at least that much by keeping it in a bank or investing it in some other way. This loss of interest is a hidden cost of your insurance that your agent will never call to your attention, but you should be aware of it as part of the total cost of your whole-life policy.

The sixth step is to add up how much your insurance premiums are each year.

Finally, add together the last two items, the annual premiums plus the interest you lose each year on your cash values. This figure is how much your insurance really costs you each year, since you literally can't afford to ignore the interest you lose on those cash values. In the "net cost" method, an agent selling you a cash-value whole-life policy will make out the cost without considering lost interest, and will "discover" that "your insurance will actually cost you nothing" in the long-run.

Let's pick a real-life example, a fellow named Peter K. Peter used to have a life policy with a giant mutual life insurance company. He paid premiums of about $400 each year, and the death benefit to his wife and daughter would have been $15,000. Now Peter and his wife are about 26 years old and have an infant daughter. How far would $15,000 have gotten his family if he had died? Maybe one year, at best. Of course, he had all those cash values piling up, but if he died, they would have vanished.

After he read a newspaper article we published on whole-life versus term insurance, Peter went to an independent agent who represented numerous companies. He found Peter a five-year level term insurance policy costing $284.50 each year which pays $100,000 if Peter dies, $18,000 on his wife, and $2000 on their child if she dies. That's quite a difference from $15,000 on Peter K's life alone! And it is costing him less when his growing family needs the protection most!

Peter, wanting an investment program as well, also decided to buy mutual funds at the rate of $29 each month, an investment which could pay off handsomely when he and his wife are ready to retire. Taken together, the term insurance and the mutual funds are cost-

A 30-YEAR-OLD MAN BUYS:

A $100,000 dividend-paying whole-life policy.

A $100,000 annual renewable term policy, converted at age 45 to a 20-year decreasing term policy, combined with a tax-sheltered annuity paying 7 percent. ($1636 in premiums is divided between the two plans.)

Annual premium including policy fee: $1636, paid for 35 years equals $57,260.

Total term insurance premiums for 35 years: $14,938. Total contribution to the annuity for 35 years: $42,322. Total cost: $57,260.

If dividends* were used to buy paid-up additions (additional whole-life insurance), the total death benefit at age 65, according to the company's computer printout, would equal $248,200.

Your death benefit at age 65 would be $305,000.

If dividends were left to accumulate at an interest rate of 6 percent you would have a death benefit at age 65 of $185,000.

If you cash in the policy at age 65, and you were buying paid-up additions, your total cash values would be $145,000.

If you live to age 65, you have in your annuity account $285,000.

Or if you choose to let dividends accumulate at interest and cash in your policy at age 65, your total cash values would be $143,000.

* Illustrated dividends are actuarial "guesstimates." They are not estimates or guarantees of future results.

ing him slightly more than the inferior whole-life insurance with cash values did, but he and his family now have financial security that his old whole-life insurance policy never offered him.

As pointed out by Sherlock Holmes, whole-life insurance can be viewed as decreasing term insurance with an increasing savings program. Of course, if you die, your beneficiary gets only the face amount of the policy, less outstanding loans. Basically, the face amount of the policy at the time of death is the sum of the then existing death protection, and savings. You can go out and buy term insurance yourself, and put your money into a separate increasing savings program. Let us show you, by doing as we just advised, how your family would fare if you died at age 65, or if you were living at age 65.

In Table E, we compare a standard low-cost dividend-paying whole-life policy issued by a leading mutual company, and a term life insurance policy, combined with a tax-sheltered annuity paying 7 percent interest. (For more about annuities, see Chapter 9, Investing Your Savings. Note to women: the same amount of insurance will cost you less, leaving more money for your savings or investment program.)

Ask yourself these three questions: (1) If you live, which would you rather have at age 65 for the same amount of money spent—$145,000 or $285,000? (2) If you die at 65, which would you rather your widow and children had for the same amount of money spent—$248,200 or $305,000? (3) Did your insurance agent show you the difference between the two plans?

Here, in Table F, is another example for a few dollars less. This time we're comparing a standard low-cost non-dividend-paying whole-life policy issued by a leading non-mutual company, and term life policy, combined with a tax-sheltered annuity paying 7 percent interest. (Again, the same amount of insurance will cost women less, freeing more money for a savings or investment plan.)

TABLE F
A 30-YEAR-OLD MAN BUYS:

A $100,000 non-dividend-paying whole-life policy.	A $100,000 annual renewable term policy, converted at age 45 to a 20-year decreasing term policy, combined with a tax-sheltered annuity paying 7 percent.
Annual premium including policy fee: $1150 for 35 years, equals $40,250.	$1150 in premiums is divided between the two plans. Total term insurance premiums for 35 years: $14,938. Total contribution to annuity for 35 years: $25,312. Total cost: $40,250.
If you die at age 65, your beneficiary gets $100,000.	Your death benefit at age 65 would be $136,000.
If you live to age 65 and cash in the policy, you get $52,250.	If you live to age 65, you would have in your annuity account $116,000.

85

Ask yourself the same three questions: (1) If you live, which would you rather have at age 65 for the same amount of money spent—$52,250 or $116,000? (2) If you die at age 65, which would you rather your widow and children had for the same amount of money spent—$100,000 or $136,000? (3) Did your insurance agent show you the difference between these two plans?

Since we're discussing costs in the short and long run, it is appropriate to mention a very specialized type of policy that is being offered which for most people is not as good as term insurance, but might be very desirable for a few people. This is called "financed" or "minimum deposit" insurance. It works this way:

The agent approaches someone who is in a 36 percent tax bracket or higher, or a person in the 28 percent tax bracket whom he flatters by telling him he will soon be in a higher tax bracket. The agent then unveils this amazing "financed insurance" concept, "a way to buy your insurance even cheaper than term insurance."

What you do is buy a whole-life policy, then several years later you borrow out the cash values, write off the interest on them as a tax loss on your income taxes, and do what you wish with the money. You must wait for several years to borrow out the cash values under the U.S. Internal Revenue Service Code, Section 264, which states that there must be "a qualification period of seven years during which four full annual premiums must be paid, no part of which is paid by means of a policy loan or indebtedness."

Agents can show you long-range projections of the costs and benefits of financed insurance that make it seem even cheaper than term insurance after several decades. There are several potential problems with financed insurance, however, which your agent will probably not emphasize. First, it only makes economic sense if you are above the 40 percent tax bracket. This insurance is often pushed on people in a lower tax bracket, mainly young professionals, who are told that they will most probably be above the 40 percent level in a few years. That's a flattering assumption. But if it doesn't happen, you could have saved money by buying term insurance.

Second, if you are in a high tax bracket, you must assume you will stay in that bracket if this plan is to save you money. Business reverses or your own illness or disability may unexpectedly throw you back in a lower tax bracket. Then, on a much lower income, you've got to pay off the interest on the cash values you've borrowed.

Also Congress might change its mind and decide to eliminate the tax deduction on interest. Tax laws are not written on stone tablets; if you want to believe that interest on insurance-policy loans will remain tax-deductible for the next several decades, that is your privilege.

You should also consider how much you would have made on your money if you had put it into other investments rather than buying insurance. Many life insurance companies are beginning to mention this hidden cost (lost interest) of whole-life insurance when they show you their cost projections. But they don't figure the lost interest into the calculations showing financed insurance to be cheaper than term, you understand. They just mention it as a footnote.

If you really need large amounts of death protection, you might not be able to afford it with this plan. Unless you have literally several thousand dollars to put into insurance each year, you won't be able to afford large amounts of death protection. You can still afford it with term, however.

Another point to consider is that the cost projections showing that financed insurance is cheaper assume that you will be getting dividends back. The company even specifies the amount of the dividends to be expected, so they can work it into the calculation to bring the ultimate price tag down. Insurance company dividends are not necessarily going to equal the projections, though. The company is not legally bound to stand by that cost projection. They don't have to pay dividends at all, if they can't or decide not to. So take the dividend projections with a grain of salt.

In the August 1977 issue of Insurance Marketing Magazine, the pitfalls of financed insurance were succinctly stated by Michael H. Levy, former chairman of the board of Standard Security Life of New York:

"Corporations and successful executives or professionals with tax levels equal to or greater than 40 percent should recognize that every dollar expended on premiums requires an earned pre-tax dollar greatly in excess of the dollar spent. Careful consideration must therefore be given to the expenditure of these premium dollars. Therein lies what is probably one of the most effective arguments in favor of term insurance in the present inflationary heavy-taxation period."

Buying financed insurance is more to your advantage in your later years, because the gap in cost between term and financed insurance is narrowing then. If you consider financed insurance, check into the rate of interest you'll have to pay on your loans. Six percent is a lot more reasonable than eight percent, over the long run.

7

Twenty Questions: A Game Your Old Agent Would Rather You Didn't Play

When your old life insurance agent calls to try to persuade you not to switch to a term policy, or to persuade you to convert the term policy he sold you to whole-life, you should answer him by asking him to give you his answers, both *in writing* and *on tape*, to the following list of questions. No agent can answer these questions honestly and still persuade you to keep or convert to whole-life insurance. Also, don't be too surprised if your old agent won't be able to answer these questions:

(1) I intend to tape-record our conversation, and your objections to my buying or keeping term insurance, so that if any false statements are made to me, I will have proof if I go to my attorney. Do you object to having your answers both recorded and on paper?

(2) Why is it to my advantage to have less insurance protection now for the same premium dollar?

(3) On a year-by-year basis, is term insurance cheaper than cash-value insurance? Please answer yes or no.

(4) If I die while I have a cash-value insurance policy in force, why doesn't my beneficiary receive my cash value in addition to the face amount?

(5) I have been told that my cash-value policy is really a decreasing term policy and a savings account that gradually places the burden of protection on me. Is this true? If not, please explain your answer.

(6) Is there ever a time that I could use my entire cash-surrender value and still have life insurance without paying interest? Please answer yes or no.

(7) Is it legal to call any portion of my cash-value policy a savings or investment plan? Yes or no?

(8) If I am gradually taking over the risk portion of my own life insurance, why is this referred to as a permanent insurance?

(9) Please give me a year-by-year breakdown of the interest I will receive on the savings portion of my cash value policy. Do not include dividends (if participating) or that portion of the current year's premium that the cash value increases by.

(10) If my cash-surrender value is really my money, why is the word surrender used?

(11) Can I get money from my cash-surrender value at any time or could an insurance company force me to wait six months? Yes or no?

(12) Please illustrate the amount of money guaranteed in comparison to the total premiums paid in. Do this on a yearly basis.

(13) Explain in detail why your answer to the previous question is a good deal for me.

(14) If the cash-surrender value is my savings, why do I have to pay an insurance company interest to use my money?

(15) Who really owns my cash-surrender value?

(16) All life insurance companies reinsure risks that exceed their limits. All the reinsurance that they purchase is yearly renewable term. Why should I purchase a sub-marginal savings account (whole-life) along with my protection?

Answer the following questions only if the policy being replaced is a participating policy, a product sold by the mutual companies which purports to pay dividends:

(17) Please explain the definition of a life insurance dividend under U.S. Treasury Decision No. 1743.

(18) If a life insurance dividend is only a partial return of a premium overcharge, why aren't dividends guaranteed, since the overcharge is guaranteed and built into the rate?

(19) Is a life insurance dividend a profit on my money? Yes or no?

(20) Why aren't life insurance dividends taxable?

8

Twenty Answers Your Old Agent Would Rather You Didn't Know

(1) An honest broker or agent will not object. Don't be surprised if a life insurance agent wedded to selling cash-value, whole-life insurance of one particular company refuses to be taped, however.

(2) Watch a less-than-candid agent squirm when he tries to answer this one. It is not to your advantage.

(3) Yes.

(4) You are insuring yourself with your cash values. They belong to the company.

(5) Yes, this is true.

(6) No.

(7) No.

(8) It will be fascinating to see how your agent tries to talk his way out of this one. In fact, this use of the word "permanent" is just insurance company jargon, as when they call term insurance "temporary"—even term-to-age-100 policies!

(9) Have your agent use a separate sheet of paper, and break it down in the same way as is shown in Table N on page 160.

(10) At the time of death, you *surrender* the cash values to the company when your beneficiary claims the death benefit.

(11) Yes, an insurance company can make you wait six months. (If you think six months is a long time, you have no idea of what might happen in the future! See Appendix A: Excerpts from the *Trend Report*, especially the parts dealing with moratoriums, page 142, for some frightening possibilities.)

(12) Use a separate sheet of paper, and break it down in the same way, again, as is shown in Table N on page 160.

(13) Of course, this isn't a good deal for you. It will be intriguing to hear the agent explain why it is, though.

(14) The money belongs to the company, not you.

(15) The company.

(16) Why, indeed? Let the agent try to explain it, but the answer is that you shouldn't.

(17) The Decision defines a "dividend" as a partial refund of a premium overcharge.

(18) If the agent is still answering these questions, the answer to this should floor you. Dividends are nothing more than actuarial guesstimates. You can't guarantee a guess.

(19) No.

(20) Unlike dividends from stocks, life insurance dividends are simply a refund of your money.

These questions—and more important, the answers—are so embarrassing for whole-life agents and companies to answer that they don't even try. Instead, in Indiana, they have succeeded in outlawing the questions. The Indiana Insurance Commissioner, H. P. Hudson, who gets his salary from taxpayer money to protect the consumers of Indiana from exploitation by insurance companies and agents, prohibited term insurance agents in his state from giving this list of questions to whole-life policyholders. H. P. Hudson sent out a bulletin to agents and companies in his state, warning them they must cease using such a form immediately or face "disciplinary action."

"On their face, many of these questions touch on subjects any worthy insurance agent should discuss with any insurance purchaser at the time of sale," Hudson was reported as saying in the *National Underwriter* on April 15, 1978. The fact is that whole-life insurance agents don't cover these points with a customer when they complete a sale, for if they did, no intelligent consumer would buy their product.

9

Investing Your Savings

Once you've cashed in your cash-surrender values on your whole-life policy, there are numerous ways you can reinvest them to get a better return on your money. The important step to take is to *commit* yourself to some program. Following are some suggestions with brief mention of the advantages and disadvantages of each. Of course, we recommend that you seek financial counseling from an independent agent or broker, one who can present numerous alternative programs, specifically tailored to your individual needs, before making a final decision.

Annuities

Annuities are the middle-income person's tax shelter, and they also have attractions for the wealthy. Although we often criticize insurance companies, we do give credit where credit is due. Term insurance is one of the worthwhile products that insurance companies offer. Now we would like to introduce the annuity, an investment alternative that a number of insurance companies offer which has the advantages of "cash values," paying higher interest rates.

Like life insurance cash values, annuities are affected by inflation, but because of their higher interest rates, which fluctuate with inflation, you are generally able to retain the purchasing power of your original investment, unlike life insurance cash values, which lose their original purchasing power.

"Annuity" is an insurance term which refers to a savings plan with unique advantages over the usual savings and thrift plans: for one thing, you can't outlive the income. It's just built into the plan that way. There are also tax benefits you just can't get any other way. More about those and other advantages after we explain the various kinds of annuities to you. (See Table G, page 99.)

(1) An *immediate annuity* is a plan by which you give the insurance company a lump sum of money within a period of a few months. Later, you start to receive payments back over a specified period of time which you and the company agree upon at the time of purchase.

(2) A *single-premium deferred annuity* is a plan in which you give the insurance company a lump sum, and payment back to you is deferred until your later years, usually at retirement.

(3) A *flexible-premium deferred annuity* is similar to a savings account at your bank. You deposit a certain amount of money each month, or quarterly or semi-annually or annually. A minimum amount, specified in your contract, is required; but as the name implies, your payment is flexible, and you can deposit more when you can afford it to make up for the times you can't.

(4) The *variable annuity* can be paid either in a lump sum or by flexible monthly premiums. However, it has an additional feature: You can designate that some portion of your contribution is to be invested in securities. This feature allows you to take advantage of the slow, general rise in the stock market over long periods of time. The taxes due on gains in the stock market are deferred until you draw your money back out of the annuity.

The insurance company takes your money and invests it in high-grade corporate bonds in stable companies. Insurance companies have certain tax advantages when they invest money, so they can pass these advantages along to you when you sign up for an annuity.

Whole-life insurance agents usually neglect to mention the annuity as an investment alternative, because the commission they receive on a high-yielding annuity with a low sales charge is a mere pittance compared with the commissions they receive on a cash-value life insurance policy. As an example, if a person put $300 into a whole-life insurance policy as opposed to a monthly annuity during the first year, the agent's commission on the whole-life would be $165, a 55 percent commission. On the other hand, the first-year commission on the annuity would be only $20 or $30, a difference which steers whole-life insurance agents away from mentioning low-cost high-interest annuities. Term agents and independent brokers often mention the annuity when they advise people to "buy term and invest the difference."

Tax Benefits That Annuities Offer

There are many tax benefits that only annuities offer.

(1) All interest income accumulates tax-free during the "deferral" period. The deferral period is the time between the original purchase date of the annuity and the date when you begin receiving payments from the annuity.

(2) The money you start the annuity with is your own money, which you've already been taxed on. Hence you never have to pay taxes again on this money, even after you begin receiving the money back. You can only be taxed on the interest you've earned, but if you are retired when you draw your interest earnings, you generally are in a lower tax bracket.

(3) No income tax is payable when death occurs during the deferral period, providing you have an annuitant who is a separate party other than the owner, and the annuitant is designated as owner/designee on the contract when purchased. An annuitant is not to be confused with a beneficiary.

(4) If the owner wishes to exchange his annuity in the future for an annuity contract with *any* other company, he may do so without being taxed on the transfer of annuity funds. So if you have an unsatisfactory annuity now, you can change to another company without being penalized by the IRS. However, to avoid taxation, you should not withdraw the cash values of the annuity yourself, but must arrange to have the company whose annuity you prefer conduct the transaction.

(5) If you die before the annuity starts to pay you back, the full contract value of the annuity is paid to your beneficiary, and you avoid the problems of probate, with its delays and legal costs, saving 4 to 8 percent, depending on where you live and on the value of the annuity.

(6) After the annuity pay-out starts, the laws of most states provide protection of both the balance of the contract and the annuity payments against the claims of creditors. Usually, you have a choice of the way in which the policy's cash values will be paid out. The methods are:

Life only. The company guarantees to pay you a prearranged monthly income for as long as you live, but the payments stop on your death. Your heirs do not receive leftover value from the annuity. Generally, this is not the best settlement to choose. Although it pays the highest monthly amount back to you, you would have to live into your eighties or nineties to "beat the odds" and collect more from the annuity than you paid into it.

Refund. This type also provides an income for life, but if you die before payments add up to the original purchase price, the company will refund the accumulated payments to your beneficiary in a lump sum or in installments.

Life and ten years certain. If you die during the first ten years after pay-out begins, the company will continue monthly payments to your beneficiary for the remainder of the ten-year period. Insurers will also guarantee payments for 15 and 20 years.

Joint and survivor. The company pays a lifetime income to two people, usually a husband and wife. The survivor may receive the same monthly income or a reduced amount, depending on the plan chosen. The policy might be available with a certain period of ten or more years beyond the annuitants' lifetime, so that payments will be made to a beneficiary after the death of the two annuitants.

Table H shows you how your investment compounds as a lump sum of $1000, $10,000, or $100,000, and how it would fare under two different interest rates. The first interest rate, of 4 percent, is the minimum lifetime interest rate guaranteed by one company. The second rate, 7¾ percent, is the rate they are actually paying at the

Table G – WHAT MAKES THE DEFERRED ANNUITY UNIQUE?

CLIENT PROFILE

- Conservative
- Older
- Substantial Means
- Safety of Principal Most Important
- Probably Disenchanted With Equities
- Tax Savings Very Important
- Wants Highest Interest Yield With Safety

PRESENT OR ALTERNATE INVESTMENT AVENUES

- Certificates of Deposit
- Commercial Paper
- Treasury Bills
- Municipal Bonds
- Corporate Bonds
- Money Market Funds
- Savings & Loans

	Guaranteed Principal	Guaranteed Earnings	Guaranteed Liquidity	Tax-Sheltered	Guaranteed Lifetime Income	Avoids Probate	"X" Factor*	"Y" Factor**
Certificates of Deposit	YES	YES	YES	NO	NO	NO	NO	NO
Savings & Loans	YES	YES	YES	NO	NO	NO	NO	NO
Commercial Paper	YES	YES	YES	NO	NO	NO	NO	NO
Treasury Bills	At Maturity YES	YES	YES	NO	NO	NO	NO	NO
Municipal Bonds	At Maturity YES	YES	YES	YES (Tax Exempt)	NO	NO	NO	NO
Corporate Bonds	At Maturity YES	YES	YES	NO	NO	NO	NO	NO
Money Market Fund	At Maturity NO	Flexible Rate	YES	NO	NO	NO	NO	NO
Annuity	YES	YES	YES	YES	YES	YES	YES	YES

* "X" Factor — is a unique feature of the annuity which allows the investor to accumulate and reinvest interest earnings without paying any current federal or state income taxes.

** "Y" Factor — allows an investor to recover his original investment during his lifetime without paying any income tax.

Table H — SINGLE PREMIUM DEFERRED ANNUITY
Cash Value Accumulations Assuming
Single Premium Deposit of:

End of Contract Year	$1,000		$10,000		$100,000	
	Guarant'd*	Total**	Guaranteed*	Total**	Guaranteed*	Total**
1	$1,040	$ 1,078	$10,400	$ 10,775	$104,000	$ 107,750
2	1,082	1,161	10,820	11,610	108,200	116,101
3	1,125	1,251	11,250	12,510	112,500	125,098
4	1,170	1,348	11,700	13,479	117,000	134,794
5	1,217	1,452	12,170	14,524	121,700	145,240
6	1,266	1,565	12,660	15,650	126,600	156,496
7	1,316	1,686	13,160	16,862	131,600	168,625
8	1,369	1,817	13,690	18,169	136,900	181,693
9	1,424	1,958	14,240	19,577	142,400	195,774
10	1,481	2,109	14,810	21,095	148,100	210,947
11	1,540	2,273	15,400	22,730	154,000	227,295
12	1,602	2,449	16,020	24,491	160,200	244,910
13	1,666	2,639	16,660	26,389	166,600	263,891
14	1,732	2,843	17,320	28,434	173,200	284,343
15	1,801	3,064	18,010	30,638	180,100	306,379
16	1,873	3,301	18,730	33,012	187,300	330,124
17	1,948	3,557	19,480	35,571	194,800	355,708
18	2,026	3,833	20,260	38,328	202,600	383,275
19	2,107	4,130	21,070	41,298	210,700	412,979
20	2,192	4,450	21,920	44,499	219,200	444,985
21	2,279	4,795	22,790	47,947	227,900	479,472
22	2,370	5,166	23,700	51,663	237,000	516,631
23	2,465	5,567	24,650	55,667	246,500	556,669
24	2,564	5,998	25,640	59,981	256,400	599,811
25	2,666	6,463	26,660	64,630	266,600	646,297
26	2,773	6,964	27,730	69,638	277,300	696,385
27	2,884	7,504	28,840	75,035	288,400	750,355
28	2,999	8,085	29,990	80,851	299,900	808,507
29	3,119	8,712	31,190	87,117	311,900	871,166
30	3,244	9,387	32,440	93,868	324,400	938,682
31	3,374	10,114	33,740	101,143	337,400	1,011,430
32	3,509	10,898	35,090	108,982	350,900	1,089,815
33	3,649	11,743	36,490	117,428	364,900	1,174,276
34	3,795	12,653	37,950	126,528	379,500	1,265,282
35	3,947	13,633	39,470	136,334	394,700	1,363,342
36	4,104	14,690	41,040	146,900	410,400	1,469,001
37	4,269	15,828	42,690	158,285	426,900	1,582,848
38	4,439	17,055	44,390	170,552	443,900	1,705,519
39	4,617	18,377	46,170	183,770	461,700	1,837,697
40	4,802	19,801	48,020	198,012	480,200	1,980,118
41	4,994	21,336	49,940	213,358	499,400	2,133,578
42	5,193	22,989	51,930	229,893	519,300	2,298,930
43	5,401	24,771	54,010	247,710	540,100	2,477,097
44	5,617	26,691	56,170	266,907	561,700	2,669,072
45	5,842	28,759	58,420	287,592	584,200	2,875,925

*Guaranteed column is the accumulations derived at the guaranteed interest rate.

**Total column is the accumulation available, including excess interest for the current interest rate being paid.

The excess interest is not guaranteed.

present time. This rate could fluctuate, of course. Observe how the money mounts up because of compound interest.

Table I is for the benefit of the working person. You can see how your earnings would build up in an annuity if you deposited $10 per month, $100 per year, or multiples thereof. The 8.5 percent administrative charge has been deducted from your contributions.

After all this saving, what do you get back? Table J shows you an example of what you could look forward to if you signed up for a flexible-premium annuity savings program.

Here's how it works. Suppose you are a retired male, 65 years old, who has accumulated $25,000. Using Table J, you see you will receive $8.20 per $1000 of accumulated annuity value. You multiply $8.20 by 25. (It's $8.20 for each $1000, and you've saved $25,000.) Your monthly income after retirement would be $205. If you had saved $100,000 over the years (which is not so difficult over a long period of time using an annuity), your monthly retirement income would be $820.

Table K shows what your pay-out would be with a single-premium deferred annuity, assuming you had put in $10,000 at certain ages. The "issue age" refers to your age when you deposited the $10,000; the "guaranteed" column shows you how much you would receive monthly if you had only earned the guaranteed minimum of 4 percent. The "total" column shows you what you would receive monthly if you had been earning at the current rate of 7¾ percent.

Administrative and sales charges vary greatly between different annuities. The best annuities are those with the lowest charges. Many single-premium deferred annuities make no sales or administrative charge against your deposit or premium, but have penalty or surrender charges for terminating early. Flexible-premium annuities (monthly or annual deposits) usually have an administrative charge of 8½ percent of the contribution, but some are currently coming onto the market that have very low or even no sales or administrative charge at all. Be sure to see what it is going to pay you, though. No sales charge on an annuity that will only pay 3 percent is foolishness. It would be better to pay a small sales charge and earn 7 to 8 percent on your contributions to your annuity.

Table I-A — Accumulated Cash Values of Flexible Premium Annuity at Various Interest Rates NET of 8.5% Sales Charge

END OF CONTRACT YEAR	ACCUMULATED VALUES* of $10 per Month at:			
	3.5%	6%	7%	8%
1	$ 111.87	$ 113.34	$ 113.92	$ 114.50
2	227.66	233.47	235.81	238.16
3	347.50	360.82	366.24	371.72
4	471.53	495.80	505.80	515.96
5	599.90	638.89	655.13	671.74
6	732.77	790.56	814.90	839.98
7	870.29	951.33	985.87	1,021.68
8	1,012.62	1,121.75	1,168.80	1,217.92
9	1,159.93	1,302.39	1,364.54	1,429.85
10	1,312.40	1,493.87	1,573.97	1,658.74
11	1,470.20	1,696.84	1,798.07	1,905.94
12	1,633.53	1,911.98	2,037.86	2,172.92
13	1,802.58	2,140.04	2,294.43	2,461.26
14	1,977.54	2,381.78	2,568.96	2,772.66
15	2,158.62	2,638.02	2,862.70	3,108.97
16	2,346.04	2,909.64	3,177.01	3,472.19
17	2,540.03	3,197.56	3,513.32	3,864.47
18	2,740.80	3,502.75	3,873.18	4,288.13
19	2,948.60	3,826.25	4,258.22	4,745.68
20	3,163.67	4,169.16	4,670.22	5,239.84
21	3,386.27	4,532.65	5,111.05	5,773.53
22	3,616.66	4,917.94	5,582.74	6,349.91
23	3,855.11	5,326.35	6,087.46	6,972.41
24	4,101.91	5,759.27	6,627.50	7,644.70
25	4,357.35	6,218.16	7,205.34	8,370.78
26	4,621.72	6,704.59	7,823.64	9,154.95
27	4,895.36	7,220.20	8,485.21	10,001.84
28	5,178.56	7,766.75	9,193.10	10,916.49
29	5,471.68	8,346.09	9,950.54	11,904.31
30	5,775.06	8,960.20	10,760.99	12,971.16
31	6,089.06	9,611.15	11,628.18	14,123.36
32	6,414.05	10,301.15	12,556.08	15,367.73
33	6,750.41	11,032.56	13,548.92	16,711.65
34	7,098.55	11,807.85	14,611.27	18,163.08
35	7,458.87	12,629.65	15,747.98	19,730.63
36	7,831.80	13,500.77	16,964.25	21,423.58
37	8,217.78	14,424.15	18,265.67	23,251.97
38	8,617.28	15,402.94	19,658.19	25,226.63
39	9,030.75	16,440.45	21,148.18	27,359.26
40	9,458.70	17,540.22	22,742.48	29,662.51
41	9,901.62	18,705.97	24,448.37	32,150.01
42	10,360.05	19,941.66	26,273.68	34,836.51
43	10,834.52	21,251.50	28,226.75	37,737.93
44	11,325.60	22,639.92	30,316.55	40,871.47
45	11,833.87	24,111.66	32,552.62	44,255.69

*Values shown are for the end of the contract year and assume premium payments are made monthly on a regular basis throughout the year. The values shown do not take into account any applicable state premium taxes.

Table I-B — Accumulated Cash Values of Flexible Premium Annuity at Various Interest Rates NET of 8.5% Sales Charge

END OF CONTRACT YEAR	ACCUMULATED VALUES** of $100 per Year at:			
	3.5%	6%	7%	8%
1	$ 94.70	$ 96.99	$ 97.90	$ 98.82
2	192.72	199.80	202.66	205.55
3	294.17	308.78	314.75	320.81
4	399.17	424.29	434.69	445.29
5	507.84	546.74	563.03	579.74
6	620.32	676.54	700.34	724.94
7	736.73	814.12	847.27	881.75
8	857.22	959.96	1,004.49	1,051.11
9	981.92	1,114.54	1,172.70	1,234.02
10	1,110.99	1,278.41	1,352.70	1,431.56
11	1,244.58	1,452.10	1,545.29	1,644.91
12	1,382.84	1,636.22	1,751.37	1,875.32
13	1,525.94	1,831.38	1,971.87	2,124.17
14	1,674.05	2,038.25	2,207.81	2,392.92
15	1,827.35	2,257.54	2,460.26	2,683.17
16	1,986.01	2,489.98	2,730.38	2,996.65
17	2,150.22	2,736.37	3,019.41	3,335.20
18	2,320.18	2,997.54	3,328.68	3,700.83
19	2,496.09	3,274.38	3,659.59	4,095.72
20	2,678.16	3,567.83	4,013.66	4,522.20
21	2,866.59	3,878.89	4,392.53	4,982.79
22	3,061.63	4,208.62	4,797.91	5,480.24
23	3,263.49	4,558.13	5,231.67	6,017.48
24	3,472.41	4,928.60	5,695.79	6,597.69
25	3,688.65	5,321.31	6,192.40	7,224.33
26	3,912.45	5,737.58	6,723.77	7,901.10
27	4,144.09	6,178.82	7,292.34	8,632.00
28	4,383.84	6,646.54	7,900.71	9,421.38
29	4,631.97	7,142.32	8,551.66	10,273.91
30	4,888.80	7,667.85	9,248.18	11,194.65
31	5,154.61	8,224.91	9,993.46	12,189.04
32	5,429.72	8,815.40	10,790.91	13,262.98
33	5,714.46	9,441.31	11,644.18	14,422.84
34	6,009.17	10,104.78	12,557.17	15,675.49
35	6,314.20	10,808.06	13,534.08	17,028.35
36	6,629.90	11,553.53	14,579.37	18,489.43
37	6,956.64	12,343.73	15,697.83	20,067.41
38	7,294.83	13,181.35	16,894.59	21,771.62
39	7,644.85	14,069.22	18,175.11	23,612.17
40	8,007.12	15,010.36	19,545.28	25,599.97
41	8,382.07	16,007.97	21,011.35	27,746.78
42	8,770.15	17,065.44	22,580.05	30,065.34
43	9,171.81	18,186.36	24,258.56	32,569.39
44	9,587.52	19,374.53	26,054.56	35,273.76
45	10,017.79	20,633.99	27,976.29	38,194.49

** Values shown are for the end of the contract year and assume the full annual premium payment is made at the beginning of the year. The values shown do not take into account any applicable state premium taxes.

Table J

Amount of Monthly Annuity Provided by $1,000 of Accumulated Flexible Premium Annuity Cash Value After Reduction for State Premium Tax, If Any. Ten Years Certain and Life Thereafter.

	ACCOUNT VALUE	60	61	62	63	64	65	66	67	68	69	70
MALES	UNDER $25,000	7.37	7.49	7.61	7.73	7.86	8.00	8.14	8.28	8.43	8.58	8.73
MALES	$25,000 OR MORE	7.57	7.68	7.80	7.93	8.06	8.20	8.34	8.48	8.63	8.78	8.94
FEMALES	UNDER $25,000	6.91	7.01	7.12	7.24	7.36	7.50	7.63	7.78	7.93	8.09	8.26
FEMALES	$25,000 OR MORE	7.10	7.21	7.32	7.44	7.56	7.69	7.83	7.98	8.13	8.30	8.46

Table K — SINGLE PREMIUM DEFERRED ANNUITY
Monthly Income for Life (10 Years Certain) Assuming:
$10,000 Single Premium at Issue Age

MALE

Issue Age	Income @ Age 60		Income @ Age 65		Income @ Age 70	
	Guarant'd*	Total**	Guarant'd*	Total**	Guarant'd*	Total**
25	$221	$1,051	$302	$1,645	$413	$2,600
26	212	976	290	1,527	397	2,413
27	204	905	279	1,417	381	2,239
28	196	840	268	1,315	367	2,078
29	189	780	258	1,221	353	1,929
30	181	724	248	1,133	339	1,790
31	174	672	239	1,051	326	1,661
32	168	623	229	976	313	1,542
33	161	579	221	906	301	1,431
34	155	537	212	840	290	1,328
35	149	498	204	780	279	1,232
36	143	462	196	724	268	1,144
37	138	429	188	672	257	1,062
38	132	398	181	624	248	985
39	127	370	174	579	238	914
40	122	343	167	537	229	849
41	118	318	161	498	220	788
42	113	296	152	463	212	731
43	109	274	149	429	203	678
44	105	255	143	398	196	630
45	101	236	138	370	188	584
46	97	219	132	343	181	542
47	93	203	127	319	174	503
48	89	189	122	296	167	467
49	86	175	118	274	161	433
50	83	163	113	255	154	402
51	79	151	109	236	148	373
52	76	140	104	219	143	346
53	73	130	100	204	137	322
54	71	121	97	189	132	298
55	68	112	93	175	127	277
56	65	104	89	163	122	257
57	63	96	86	151	117	239
58	60	90	82	140	113	221
59	58	83	79	130	108	205
60			76	121	104	191
61			73	112	100	177
62			70	104	96	164
63			68	96	93	152
64			65	90	89	141
65					86	131
66					82	122
67					79	113
68					76	105
69					73	97

*Guaranteed monthly income is the income derived from the total cash available at the guaranteed annuity rate.

**Total monthly income is the total income available, including excess interest, for the current annuity rate being paid.

Neither the excess interest nor the current annuity rate is guaranteed.

To sum it up, it is imperative that you demand a statement from the company which clearly shows the exact amount of sales or administrative charges made against your annuity or premium, what the annuity will pay back to you currently (if you wish) or at maturity and how much money, as well as interest, you will have in your account on a yearly basis.

You might want to consider getting a *waiver-of-premium* rider on your annuity in case, for some reason, you couldn't continue payments, and providing the rider is not too expensive. This could be especially useful if you had no disability income insurance, and became disabled.

Annuities, of course, are really for long-term investment. If you think you may need money within the next few years, you would be wise to carefully investigate the surrender charges of the annuity you are considering. You may be better off putting the money in a bank, savings and loan, or a credit union, where it is instantly available to you at no or little charge.

The following companies can be contacted to obtain the types of annuities we've discussed.

American General Life
   Insurance Company
2727 Allen Parkway
Houston, Texas 77019
(A+ excellent)

Anchor National Life Insurance
   Company
Camelback at 22nd St.
Phoenix, Arizona 85016
(A+ excellent)

Capitol Life Insurance Co.
1600 Sherman St.
Denver, Colorado 80203
(A excellent)

Fireman's Fund American Life
   Insurance Company
1600 Los Gamos Dr.
San Rafael, California 94911
(A+ excellent)

Great American Life Insurance
   Company
P.O. Box 30019
Los Angeles, California 90030
(A excellent)

Life Insurance Company of North
   America
1600 Arch St.
Philadelphia, Pennsylvania 19101
(A+ excellent)

Manufacturer's Life Insurance
   Company
200 Bloor St. East
Toronto, Ontario, Canada
   M4W 1E4
(A+ excellent)

North American Company for Life
and Health
Box 466
Chicago, Illinois 60690
(A+ excellent)

United Investors Life Insurance
Co.
One Crown Center
P.O. Box 1441
Kansas City, Missouri 64141
(A+ excellent)

Washington National Insurance Co.
1630 Chicago Ave.
Evanston, Illinois 60201
(A+ excellent)

Western National Life Insurance
Company
205 East 10th St.
Amarillo, Texas 79101
(A+ excellent)

TABLE L
HYPOTHETICAL EXAMPLES OF $10,000 ACCOUNTS

No. of Years	$10,000 Savings & Loan Accounts at 7½% Interest (Interest taxed as accrued)		$10,000 Single Premium Annuity (Interest accumulates without current tax)
	50% Tax Bracket	30% Tax Bracket	@ 8% *
5	$12,021	$12,916	$13,547
10	14,450	16,681	19,906
15	17,371	21,544	29,247
20	20,882	27,825	42,974
25	25,102	35,938	63,143
30	30,175	46,416	92,779
35	36,273	59,948	136,323
40	43,604	77,426	200,303

* Assumes level 8% interest throughout life of contract.

Before leaving the subject of annuities, here is another plan which has gained favor among knowledgeable investors.

The *Swiss franc annuity* is a sophisticated way of increasing the benefits of tax deferral. When you buy such an annuity, you use dollars to buy Swiss francs, a gold-backed currency which has been increasing in value relative to the declining dollar. The theory is that in future years, because of the appreciating Swiss franc, you will get back more dollars and will have been able to hedge against inflation in America. The Swiss franc annuity is available in limited amounts and markets. Registered investment advisers can help you decide if this type of annuity is for you. Even though it is available only from Swiss insurance companies, it can be purchased in the United States.

Other Investment Possibilities

Banks, savings and loans, and *credit unions* all pay higher rates of interest than life insurance policies, and you don't have to "borrow" your own money back and pay interest on it if you need it; all you have to do is make a withdrawal. It is easy to set up an account, too. Unfortunately, the interest earned on these accounts is taxable every year.

Stocks and *bonds* and *mutual funds* are for more confident, investment-prone people. Almost everybody knows about the risks and opportunities offered by the stock market, but fewer people understand mutual funds. Mutual funds are a group of stocks and bonds that are pooled together, thus avoiding the risk of putting all your money into just one or two stocks. The usual monthly purchase price for mutual fund shares is $25 or more. Mutual funds are generally considered to be long-term investment programs, taking advantage of the ups and downs of the stock market. This is done with "dollar-cost averaging," a method that buys fewer shares when prices are higher, but more shares when prices are lower. This results in a reduction of the purchase price for a shareholder. A well-managed mutual fund offers a chance to hedge against inflation and the opportunity for real wealth by investing in industry.

Tax-exempt municipals are a means of investing and getting tax-free present income that is often higher than after-tax returns on other securities which provide far less safety of principal. Interest on municipal bonds has been exempt from federal income taxes since 1913, and generally from taxes of the state in which they are issued.

However, an increase in public funds used to buy municipal bonds has lowered their yield, so they have little advantage over taxable investments with a higher return. In short, only people in fairly high tax brackets stand to gain by investing in municipal bonds.

Today in many of our metropolitan areas, you will find registered investment advisers who specialize in selected mutual funds and *market timing*. We are referring to that group that is registered with the Securities and Exchange Commission and have met the necessary qualifications to call themselves registered investment advisers. We are not referring to those in the insurance or securities business who refer to themselves as investment advisers simply because they dispense investment advice.

For a small annual fee, these registered advisers will advise you as to which mutual fund is well suited for your investment objectives at the time you invest. Then they will provide you with continuing market-timing information, as to where, in their opinion, your money should be invested in the future. For example, they might advise you to make an initial investment in government securities or a money mutual fund because they anticipate that the value of stocks in general will decline in the immediate future. Then, when they anticipate that the value of stocks will rise, they might advise you to move your money into a more aggressive mutual fund. Some advisers might recommend many moves within a year. Others may recommend moves only when the basic trend of the market appears to be changing. A successful adviser's timing will have your dollars in stocks in a rising market. When the market is falling, he'll have your dollars in a money position earning interest.

This type of market timing can be very appropriate for those with individual retirement accounts or HR-10 "Keogh" plans (an individual retirement account for the self-employed) and for corporate pension or profit-sharing plans.

These plans accumulate earnings on a tax-deferred basis, but market timing is also used by individuals outside tax shelters. Keep in mind that earned interest and short-term capital gains are subject to ordinary income tax in the year in which they are earned, when no tax-sheltered plan is involved.

Many investment advisers work only with no-load (a "load" is a sales charge) or low-load mutual funds to keep your costs at a minimum. In addition, if you prefer, some advisers work with individual securities. Keep in mind that an adviser must be successful to keep his clientele. Ask to see his track record.

Individual retirement accounts (IRA's) were designed for people who don't already have some kind of pension plan where they work. In brief, the government allows you to contribute up to 15 percent of your income, up to a maximum of $1500 each year, to an individual retirement account which is tax-free until you cash it in at retirement, when your tax rate is generally lower.

Money you put aside for an IRA can be put into a bank account, an insurance annuity, mutual funds, or government bonds. More complete information on IRA's can be received from financial counselors, or by writing to the Pension Benefit Guaranty Corporation, 2020 K St. N.W., Washington, D.C. 20006, Attention: Department of Communications. Ask for the IRA booklet. Single copies are free.

Self-employed people can qualify for IRA accounts if they wish, but they also have the option to participate in a "Keogh" plan, which allows up to $7500 a year in contributions to an IRA-style account.

Durable goods, from antiques to real estate, can be good or bad investments. Coins, stamps, antiques, and real estate all tend to rise in value, but you do have to know the market you are in. If you already have a mortgage on your home with high interest, you can use your cash-surrender values to pay it off early and save a great deal of interest on the loan. If you have a small business, you can invest in your own business rather than in an outside investment. Home improvements are a tangible investment and are enjoyable while they increase the value of your property. The list of possibilities is endless; you just have to count on finding a buyer willing to pay your price when the time comes for you to cash in on your investment.

The effects of inflation also have to be accounted for. Let's suppose you can now live comfortably on $1,000 a month, and you plan to retire in ten years. In order to maintain your standard of living, you'll need $2,000 to live just as well ten years from now if inflation continues to average 7 to 9 percent or more annually.

Cash-surrender value whole-life insurance policies eventually will be driven off the market by inflation, if not by other forces, because the interest one gets on the cash values doesn't even keep up with inflation. *You are actually financing your own poverty by putting your money into cash-value insurance policies,* and it appears that those policies might be partially responsible for the fact that today half the retired couples in America aged 65 and over have annual incomes of less than $5000 and only one third have incomes over $7000. Sooner or later, the public will realize that cash values—which only pay sub-marginal interest rates when inflation is racing along at 7 to 9 percent annually—are a bad buy no matter how slick the agent's sales pitch is. (For the utterly destructive impact of inflation—on whole-life insurance companies as well as whole-life policyholders—see Appendix A: Excerpts from the *Trend Report,* page 135.)

CHART D

Purchasing Power of the U.S. Dollar 1951–1976

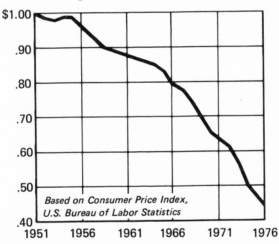

In the past 25 years, the U.S. dollar has lost over half of its purchasing power as the cost of living has more than doubled.

Points to remember about investments:

(1) The devastating effect of inflation must be taken into consideration for all investments.

(2) Diversification of investments reduces risks.

(3) Professional management reduces risks.

(4) Tax-sheltered returns increase capital available for reinvestment, thus compounding growth.

(5) Each investment selected must be compatible with one's investment objective.

(6) Investment expenditures must provide maximum returns consistent with stated risks.

10
Women Be Wise

Many women reading this book are probably either homemakers or the family breadwinners, and we have a special message to both.

If you are a single woman or the head of your own family, be forewarned that insurance companies are now looking to single women as a ripe market for cash-value policies. Magazines such as *Life Insurance Selling* have been featuring extremely patronizing articles advising insurance agents to seek out women and sell them insurance. These articles advise the agent to pretend to be interested in you as a person, to avoid any controversial subjects (like the women's movement), and to use anything you say as an opening for a sales pitch to buy some insurance.

Already the Pioneer Western Corporation has discovered that single women hold 7.5 percent of all insurance policies, and 50 percent more women hold policies than six years ago. Unfortunately, most of these women have cash-value policies, since the Pioneer study found that they plan to use their cash values for "travel, expenses of unforeseen illnesses, or retirement." Women who do use their policies for such expenses will soon discover the rate of interest they must pay to borrow back their money, but they may not realize that they are reducing the death benefit of the policy by the amount they borrow.

Single women or family breadwinners, take care! In all cases, be sure to get enough insurance to see your family through their years of need. You'll have to buy term insurance to be able to afford adequate protection and security.

Women who are shopping for term insurance should remember that they live longer than men; consequently they should expect to pay less for term insurance than would a man of the same age. Many insurance companies offer women rates equal to those of a man three years younger. This is good, but it still is outright over-charging in the guise of a discount; the latest mortality tables clearly show that women should be charged rates equal to a man seven years younger.

One of the best ways that a breadwinner can provide for the family's security is to leave a will directing how the family's money is to be distributed. The life insurance industry's "Widow's Study" found that only 29 percent of husbands left wills to assure that there would be no problems over who had a claim on the estate. When there is no will, relatives often contend for the money, causing more problems for the surviving family. Also, a will can be used to set up a trust fund so that the family will receive their benefits over a period of time; then nobody can swindle the sur-viving family out of their money. It's an excellent idea for the provider of the family to discuss with an attorney how to draw up a will, and how it can be used to provide for the survivors after his or her death.

As for homemakers, they should be concerned about what type of policies their husbands may already own. The wife is most directly affected after the death of the husband, and would obviously rather receive a benefit check for $100,000 than for $10,000. How can anyone think of leaving a wife and children behind with only $10,000, when they can be insured for three to ten times as much for the same amount of money, depending upon the insured's age? The insurance companies and their agents have left many thousands of families in poverty by pushing cash-value life insurance policies on husbands; don't let your family be the next. Ask your husband to examine his policy; talk to him about this matter if his insurance program doesn't provide enough protection and security for you and the children. Then it's time to make some immediate changes.

To add insult to injury, after the husband's death the agent will return again and again, hounding the poor widow to buy more worthless cash-value life insurance on herself and her children to provide a sort of burial fund "just in case." Or if the agent is from the Aetna Life and Casualty Co., he may try persuading the widow that she should leave 90 percent of the death benefit in the company's hands, so they can handle her money "until she is emotionally ready to make" decisions about her future. This new gimmick for keeping the widow's money in the company coffers was reported in the March 4, 1978, issue of *National Underwriter*.

In an emotional state of mind, a widow may not realize that if the agent had done his job properly there would be no need for him to return again and again. Anyone can afford term insurance that will pay $100,000, particularly at younger ages, and the agent knows this. The agent, however, made his commissions on his visits to the husband, and now he'll return in hopes of making another sale to (and commission from) the widow.

Women ought to be particularly incensed with the life insurance industry in America for being one of the last and most powerful bastions of sexism in our society. Along with the banking industry, insurance is a "men only" club at the decision-making levels, dedicated to skimming money off women clients while oppressing their female workers. Ask your insurance agent, for example, who the women are in the top management of his company. In almost every one of the 1800-plus insurance companies, even the supposedly policyholder-managed mutuals, top management is a closed male society. (We are aware of only one insurance company in America run by women. Unfortunately, it is not aggressively marketing low-priced term insurance.)

Not that the companies don't hire women; they cram their secretarial and sales forces with women who are paid substandard wages to serve as the foot soldiers of insurance exploitation and sexism. Ask the president of your insurance company, though, what his position is on the Equal Rights Amendment, and listen for his reply. The ERA would require the insurance companies to eliminate discrimination in pay and promotion, so the industry generally opposes it. ERA will increase costs, and thus raise the cost of the policies, they cry. Such concern for the policyholder would almost sound

115

sincere if the companies weren't already raising costs to the policy-holders by paying for cavernous offices and other "perks" for their (predominantly) male management forces.

If you are reading this, and are incensed, don't go away; there's more.

In 1970, the Life Underwriter Training Council and the Life Insurance Agency Management Association (LUTC and LIAMA) published the results of a study conducted in 1968 and 1969 on 1744 widows of men who died unexpectedly through illness or accident. While the "Widow's Study" was written and presented in such a way as to present the insurance companies in the best possible light, it revealed that the insurance industry has done a remarkably poor job of providing for the survivors of the insured. Among other things, the "Widow's Study" found:

The median age for the dead husbands was 56. The median age for women who became widows was 52.

"The widows rated family members and attorneys as being the most helpful persons with whom they dealt. Life insurance men were low on the list, and were in the middle of a group that included clergymen, social security officials, bankers, and union representatives."

"Ninety-two percent of the widows said that their husbands had some form of life insurance ... only 7 percent received monthly benefit payments from income options or annuities."

The majority of the widows (52 percent) received less than $5000 in death benefits, and 70 percent received less than $10,000.

"One-half of the widows said that their living standards had declined following the death of their husbands, and 1 in every 5 described her living standards as being much lower than before."

"Almost half of the families (47%) had dependent children, and 37% of the widowed mothers said that their financial situations had had an effect on their children's lives, 13% saying that the plans for their children's education had been, or would be, affected ..."

Less than one widow in five ever discussed insurance with her husband.

"Work, rather than being freely chosen, too often has been forced upon the widow by economic necessity, perhaps even before she has had an opportunity to develop the skills that would enable her to work most effectively."

Only "one-fourth of the widows said that an agent had prepared a program outlining her husband's insurance needs."

The "Widow's Study" sums up the performance of the life insurance industry quite succinctly: "The fact that a wife faces a 50-50 chance of undergoing a decline in living standards if her husband dies prematurely—and a one-in-five chance of undergoing a serious decline—should dispel any complacency about the adequacy of existing life insurance benefits."

Poor widows! The tremendous amounts of money reportedly coming into the companies' coffers through this operation—and the small amounts being paid in benefits to survivors—indicates that the policies in question were whole-life. If only their husbands had bought adequate amounts of term insurance instead of being suckered into whole-life contracts. And while these widows were counting their pennies and wondering how they'd send Billy and Susie to college, or just pay the rent, where were their agents?

For exactly where the most successful agents are, see Appendix B: The Million Dollar Round Table, on page 146.

(For an excellent study of widow's problems, we recommend the book *Widow*, by Lynn Caine, available in paperback from Bantam Books.)

11

The Conspirators in Court

If you really think you've been had, that your agent sold you a very high cost policy which didn't provide large enough death benefits at too high a cost, you might consider suing him. In 1958, Robert I. Knox succeeded in suing his insurance agent, J. Leland Anderson, for more than $25,000. Anderson had sold Knox a policy which had an annual premium of $7265 at a time when Knox's annual income was only $8100! If your agent represents himself as an "expert" or "consultant" and sells you a bad policy, he is also legally responsible. If you tell him you want the biggest death benefit for the least cost and he fails to advise you about term insurance, and sells you cash-value whole-life insurance, you also may have a claim against him. It's unlikely that your agent has taken you for a ride like that, but if you are extremely dissatisfied with the performance of your insurance agent, see a lawyer about it.

If you want to investigate this possibility, take all your policies and all the tables, graphs, "dividend projections," and other materials you received to an attorney. You might want to get copies from your agent, if necessary. Your attorney can advise you whether your case is strong enough to pursue.

While you might be able to successfully sue an agent for insurance malpractice, it's just about impossible to bring federal legal action against the companies successfully. In 1972, Mr. William

Steingart brought suit on behalf of all mutual insurance policy-holders against those four companies that, he said, were representative of mutual companies in America.

Steingart alleged that the mutual insurance companies had fixed their prices at high levels; that they used questionable accounting procedures; that they pooled vast reserves of money in funds, executive benefits, and non-insurance ventures unjustifiably; and that the directors and the officers of the companies thwarted "every semblance of corporate democracy" by perpetuating their control of the companies.

Judge Metzner ruled, however, that Mr. Steingart didn't have a leg to stand on, legally speaking. A 1945 law entitled the McCarran-Ferguson Act says, in part: "(b) No Act of Congress shall be construed to invalidate, impair, or supersede any law enacted by any state for the purpose of regulating the business of insurance . . ." It was a simple matter for the insurance companies' attorneys (hired and paid for, by the way, with the policyholders' money) to persuade Judge Metzner that the mutual insurance companies were regulated at the state level, therefore federal anti-trust laws did not apply to them. Steingart's case was dismissed, and his evidence relating to price-fixing and the perpetuation of the leadership of the mutual companies was never heard before the court. Steingart's only chance would have been to show that the state regulation was "mere pretense"; however, he was unprepared to do so.

Although William Steingart lost his revolutionary case against all the mutuals, other people with more limited, specific grievances have won suits against the insurance companies.

Tom Venegas of California worked for Prudential, selling the company's cash-value product. While working for Prudential, he'd apparently been considered a respected agent. But somewhere along the way he quit the giant company, and eventually began replacing his clients' cash-value policies with term insurance.

What happened next, said Mr. Venegas, was that Prudential's "improperly trained and misguided agents" began a "vicious personal attack" against him, attempting to discredit him with his clients.

Tom Venegas took both the giant company and its agents to court, charging them with "interfering with his contractual business" and attempting to "discredit" him. In a unanimous decision, the California Superior Court awarded him $36,500 in compensatory damages and $85,000 in punitive damages.

12

Protecting the Consumer: The Federal Trade Commission Meets the Industry Head-On

Senator Philip A. Hart, who led the Senate subcommittee investigations and hearings on life insurance abuses, was the toughest opponent the insurance industry ever faced. His findings led him to introduce a "truth-in-life-insurance" bill (See Appendix D: Synopsis of Senate Bill 2065—Truth-in-Life-Insurance, page 159), drafted by Dean Sharp. However, the death of Senator Hart and the slow suffocation of the bill ended close examination and criticism of the life insurance companies—but only temporarily. Hart and Sharp exposed cost differences between policies and industry abuses so thoroughly that other agencies picked up their banner.

The most serious recent challenge came from the staff of the Federal Trade Commission (FTC), which wanted the insurance agent to provide his client prior to any sale, with the kind of information which would help him choose between term and whole-life.* The point is, with whole-life insurance, you get a very poor

* In a prepared statement before a U.S. Congressional Committee, August 7, 1978, Albert Kramer, Director of the Bureau of Consumer Protection, FTC, said: "For every whole-life policy [consumers] are shown they should receive information about (a) the rate of return they would receive on the savings element of that policy; (b) approximately how much of the premium of that policy will go for death benefits and how much will go into savings; and (c) the severe economic consequences of early termination of that policy."

rate of return on the money you pay in. What you must count as part of the cost of the whole-life policy is the money you've lost by not investing or saving it elsewhere where you can get a decent rate of interest on your dollars.

Senator Hart and Dean Sharp found that costs between similar cash-value contracts, sold by different companies, varied by as much as 300 percent. The FTC staff, which took over the voluminous files that Hart and Sharp compiled, confirmed their revelations. The copy of the *FTC News* dated December 15, 1976, which announced the formal FTC investigation into policy pricing, noted:

> Preliminary information available to the Commission's staff suggests that the cost to consumers for essentially the same life-insurance protection varies greatly. Examination of differences in costs of popular $25,000 whole-life insurance policies issued in 1972, for example, reveals that a purchaser could save thousands of dollars over a 20-year period by buying a low-, rather than high-cost policy and still receive the same benefits.
>
> The apparently large variation in cost for similar insurance policies may be the result of inadequate cost-comparison information being furnished to prospective purchasers and a tendency on the part of buyers in the absence of adequate cost information to equate "premium" and "cost."
>
> The cost of a policy is essentially the difference between what the purchaser pays and what the purchaser gets back, and involves more than just the size of the premium.
>
> To compute the cost of a policy it is necessary to not only consider the size of premiums but to look at dividends and cash values (in policies that have them), and to make adjustments to take into account that money is paid and received at different times. Policies with the same annual premium often differ substantially in cost, depending primarily on their dividend scales, and the growth of their cash values.
>
> If consumers bought lower cost policies, potential savings on life-insurance purchases could be very large. Americans paid over 29 billion dollars in life-insurance premiums in 1975. This represented 2.72 percent of the total disposable personal income available in that year.

Worst of all for the companies, the FTC staff is considering a national "shopper's guide" to life insurance, rating policies the same way the tar-nicotine content of cigarettes and the gas mileage of automobiles are disclosed. Some quotations from the proposed guide show just how tough the FTC was making it:

> Not all agents are well-informed. Not all policies are competitively priced. And not all agents are free to offer you choices that are in your best interests because they may represent only one high-cost company . . .
>
> The point to remember is that a renewable term policy, and not just a whole life policy, can meet your long-term insurance needs at least through age 65. Therefore, if you're just interested in getting the most death protection for your money, buy term insurance. . . .
>
> Before you purchase . . . any . . . whole life policy, you should seriously consider whether your insurance needs can be better met by having term insurance. . . . [i]f you're not interested in using life insurance as a way to save, buy term insurance.

Michael Lynch, the chief economist of the FTC study, thinks that if these measures are adopted nationally, agents may revolt against their companies when they realize what they've been doing to their clients. "I believe a substantial portion of the agents have no idea how they are screwing their friends and families," said Lynch in a public statement. "It may be a whisper in their heads that they're not doing their friends a favor by selling them a certain policy, but if the federal government insists on explicit price information, it will be harder to rationalize that they are doing something good; they will lose their missionary zeal."

On the surface, the life insurance lobbyists shrugged the whole attack off with typical callousness. "They [the FTC] would be dangerous if they knew what they were doing," commented Robert Waldron, of the American Council of Life Insurance, to Jean Carper, an experienced consumer affairs writer for the Washington *Post*. Waldron was just whistling past the graveyard, though. In fact, the American Council of Life Insurance was alarmed enough to move its staff of 100 from New York to Washington, D.C., to more effectively lobby against the FTC move.

The industry has the money to employ some of the best legal and political minds in America, and they didn't just sit on their hands, or cash reserves, or whatever, waiting for the FTC to spoil their game. The McCarran-Ferguson Act exempts the industry from any federal regulation in matters which the states already regulate. In 1974, NAIC, the National Association of Insurance Commissioners, came up with an industry-supported price "disclosure" plan which they tried to ram through the state governments.

The NAIC plan is so weak as to be laughable. The agent doesn't have to present any price comparisons nor any rate-of-return data on the savings portion of the whole-life policy. He only has to give the consumer a cost figure for the policy he buys. Hence, the consumer has nothing to compare that price with, or any way to tell whether he should choose term over whole life in the first place. Furthermore, the price disclosure isn't made until *after* the sale is closed. The client could cancel the policy and buy another in order to try and locate a cheaper policy, but frankly, how many consumers will bother to do this, particularly when state replacement regulations purposely discourage switching policies? The NAIC "alternative" is cost disclosure in name only.

The American Council of Life Insurance succeeded in persuading several states to adopt the NAIC model system—states which do not have shining reputations for protecting their consumers. Then its Washington lobbyists went to work on the House and Senate Appropriations Committees, which approve the budget for the FTC.

What happens when a federal agency, determined on reform, meets an industry determined to protect its privileges?

In June 1978, FTC Chairman Michael Pertschuk announced that there would be no FTC trade regulation rules governing insurance cost disclosure—at least through the fiscal year 1979. The reason? The House and Senate Appropriations Committees, guided by the American Council of Life Insurance, inserted language in its FTC budget Appropriation Report which "directs that in no event should the commission nor its staff attempt to impede or thwart the adoption by the states of the model life insurance cost solicitation regulation supported by the NAIC." In short, the FTC is forbidden from even holding hearings on "the sacred cow," life insurance.

But the FTC hasn't abandoned the struggle entirely. Staff members have told these authors that the guidebook and regulations will come. It's just a matter of time, they feel, until the public and Congress are finally able to resist the life insurance industry's political offensive. Perhaps after the next election season is over . . .

To the detriment of the public, the companies continue to lobby their way out of some extremely tight corners, and have avoided real regulation in America since their founding. The life insurance industry has amassed in excess of $350 billion in assets. Most of these billions are owned by the mutual insurance giants—who proclaim that America's policyholders actually own this wealth. Unfortunately, the unsuspecting and unorganized policyholders cannot gain control of these self-perpetuating bastions of power. At their annual meetings, only a handful of enlightened policyholders, out of millions, dare to show up to challenge the smug company executives, who view themselves as the righteous guardians of the policyholders' wealth! These giant companies, with their wasteful and inefficient cash-value products, continue to reign as a quiet, menacing monopoly over the lives and fortunes of innocent policyholders and their families.

13

Death and Taxes

Death and taxes are proverbially the two inescapable consequences of life. A bit of planning, however, can lessen the disruptive effects of taxes, and make life more bearable for the survivors.

Whether you buy whole-life or term insurance, the money the survivor receives will not be taxed as income. Estate (or inheritance) taxes, however, apply to both types of insurance.

Careful planning with a lawyer can minimize estate taxes. Also consider assigning ownership of your life policies to your spouse or beneficiary, a move which could help avoid taxes. Group coverage, as well as individual policies, can usually be assigned.

But be careful. Assignment may be irrevocable. In the event of a divorce, the policy isn't yours, so you can't change the beneficiary. Caution suggests assigning only late in life, but, to avoid adverse federal tax consequences, not "in contemplation of death" (there's a three-year "presumption" for this) and only with your lawyer's advice.

For a more exhaustive discussion of taxation of life insurance proceeds, get the book *The Tax Companion*, an easy-to-read guidebook, from R & R Newkirk Publications, Box 1727, Indianapolis, Indiana 46206, $2 plus postage.

There are charts and tables that are guides to federal estate and gift tax rates, and estate-settlement costs, but they are difficult to read and understand without explicit directions. Ask your tax agent, broker, or financial adviser to get you one—and to explain it to you.

There is one important way to avoid estate taxes—by taking advantage of what is called "the marital deduction." For example, the tax laws say the marital deduction may not exceed 50 percent of the "adjusted estate" or $250,000, whichever is greater. The "adjusted gross estate" is the total estate minus allowable deductions for funeral expenses, estate-administration expenses, debts of the deceased, and certain allowable losses. Here is an example of how it works:

TABLE M

Value of gross estate	$370,000
Deductions	
Funeral expenses	$ 5,000
Administrative expenses	$ 40,000
Debts of deceased	$ 75,000
Total deductions	$120,000
From gross estate	$370,000
Subtract total deductions	$120,000
And you are left with	$250,000

In this example, the maximum allowable marital deduction would be $250,000 if the *entire* estate passed on to the surviving spouse. Of course, if the adjusted gross estate had equaled a million dollars, and the widow was the *sole* beneficiary, 50 percent of the estate ($500,000) would have been the higher figure. But let's go back to our first example for a moment. If the estate had been divided between the spouse, say, and the children, something else would have happened. The spouse would have gotten $125,000—which would not have been subject to estate taxes because of "the marital deduction." The $125,000 going to the children, however, would be taxed.

Billions of dollars of life insurance is sold to people who are trying to minimize estate taxes. As we have shown, however, *there are legal ways of avoiding these taxes without buying any kind of life insurance.* You'd be well advised to confer with your attorney on this, unless you enjoy paying insurance premiums needlessly.

14
ꞌIn Conclusion

Complete reform of the life insurance industry will require more than just the passage of a national "truth-in-life-insurance" bill. To completely clean up this giant menacing monopoly operating under the protective canopy of state regulation, a number of additional measures will be required.

Full financial disclosure within the industry will be necessary, ranging from totally opening up the books and records of the mutual insurance companies all the way down to rewriting the policies and contracts so that people can easily understand them. At the highest levels, this would expose gross waste, poor management, and any illegal or irregular activities by executives or organized crime, at lower levels, it would make the workings of the insurance industry understandable to most people.

Insurance buyers can do themselves, their families, and other consumers a favor by resisting high-pressure and misleading sales practices and by reporting the agent and the company he works for to their state insurance commissioner and the Federal Trade Commission. Most people don't even realize the state insurance office exists to "protect" them, so they never report abuses even when they are angry about them. The state insurance commissioners may help the companies reform if they think there is a groundswell for federal regulation. The commissioners, after all, don't want to find themselves out of a job.

Don't get your hopes up too high when contacting the state insurance commissioner, though. The state commissioners are linked into the National Association of Insurance Commissioners (NAIC), which exists primarily to help the insurance companies carry on their business. If you run across the *NAIC Insurance Buyer's Guide*, for example, don't be fooled into buying an expensive whole-life policy. As we've seen, the NAIC guide is actually a weak attempt to head off real price disclosure such as the Federal Trade Commission is advocating. The NAIC guide should be called what it is: "A Seller's Guide."

State Insurance Departments should design a disclosure system which would require every life insurance company to provide *prospective* buyers with rates-of-return on the savings portion of any life policy containing cash values. Said disclosure should, by law, be made before any sale is completed.

This proposed disclosure system should replace the industry-sponsored model which the NAIC is currently huckstering. If the State Insurance Departments or State Legislatures refuse to adopt an adequate rate-of-return disclosure system, then Congress must enact national truth-in-life-insurance legislation.

Insurance agents should be required to consider the value of the lost interest on cash values when figuring the cost of insurance, and should be required to explain policies in easy-to-understand graphs, illustrations, and brochures that aren't biased in favor of whole-life insurance. Agents must receive better training in financial matters, with less emphasis on salesmanship. Financial planners and independent insurance brokers and agents, not the present group of whole-life-oriented Chartered Life Underwriters, should teach insurance. Consumers would benefit greatly by seeking out independent agents and brokers and especially to avoiding captive life agents, representing one company only, who push whole-life policies. The commission system of paying agents and brokers has to be changed to provide sufficient monetary incentive to sell low-cost term insurance, and thus end the temptation for them to recommend high-cost low-protection cash-value insurance for the same cost as term insurance.

It is very important for you to take the time to shop around before

129

buying any life insurance policy. Give your insurance shopping the same time and care you'd give to buying a new car. After all, your insurance is a much more basic need, and a much bigger expenditure. If you don't have the time or inclination to shop around, have an independent insurance broker or agent find a low-cost term policy that will suit your needs. Remember, the captive insurance agent works for his company, but your independent insurance broker works for *you*.

If you are getting rid of a costly whole-life policy as a result of reading our book, why not call up your own Agent Abernathy and ask him over for a heart-to-heart talk? Find out just what he was thinking of when he sold you your whole-life policy. Have him answer the twenty questions listed in the book while he's there.

Consumers and future consumers should receive better education in financial matters in high school and college, and from the newspapers and other media. The vast sums of money that insurance companies pour into the media in the form of full-page ads and commercials may make it difficult for the media to respond to this need, but the schools could set up courses on financial planning which would cover insurance and other topics. The schools would have to be wary of insurance companies that offered to prepare texts and lectures on insurance, however.

Insurance agents and brokers selling individual life insurance policies should be freed from anti-rebate laws which prohibit them from competing by cutting their commissions directly to the client. This step alone would save consumers millions of dollars annually. Agents, independent or otherwise, are paid fixed rates for their services. To accept less or give some back would lose the agent his or her license. Every time such anti-competitive laws are repealed, consumer prices drop. Large group insurance cases are issued on a negotiated commission basis. Why not allow agents and brokers selling individual policies to do the same?

Repeal of the McCarran-Ferguson Act would immediately open the life insurance companies up to the full scope of federal antitrust laws. Brokers who sell stocks, mutual funds, and securities are subject to reasonable federal disclosure regulation by the Securities and Exchange Commission. For example, a broker who sells you securities that are not suited to your financial situation can lose his license. Why shouldn't life insurance agents, who claim to be selling you "guaranteed security" be bound by similar federal regulations?

Senators, Congresspersons and the public must finally wake up to the fact that there is no moral justification for jeopardizing the welfare and security of the family simply because the life insurance industry and its agents are more concerned with their profits than the policyholders' well-being. The best way to fight the life insurance conspiracy is to buy what is best for you and your family —and not wait to be "sold" what is best for the agent and the company.

But most of all, live long and prosper.

'Waste, Overcharging' Alleged

...ator Aims to Shake Up Life Insu...

By ANN McFEATTERS
Scripps-Howard Staff Writer

WASHINGTON. — Sen. Philip A. Hart, D-Mich., who aroused the country over auto insurance scandals, now says he has uncovered "waste, inefficiency and overcharging" in the life insurance industry.

He will introduce a truth-in-life-insurance bill which is certain to cause as much scurrying in that industry as his no-fault auto insurance

b 24-A **THE MIAMI HERALD**

analysis of a survey of 200 life insurance companies which they say proves consumers pay too much for too little protection.

The main problem, Hart's aides say, is that even simple concepts of life insurance buying have been made so fuzzy consumers don't understand what their premiums pay for.

"Life insurance buyers need — and are not getting-clear, accurate, reliable and adequate information about

Wed., Feb. 21, 1973 value of the

the Association for Advanced Life Underwriting.

This charge has been echoed by various critics, including Virginia H. Knauer, President Nixon's consumer specialist, and the National Association of (State) Insurance Commissioners.

An investigation by the Senate antitrust and monopoly subcommittee has found that:

• Policyholders lost millions of dollars a year because they terminate some policies too soon to collect payments in stocks or a su...

• Comp... is not re... consume... insuranc... policies... dreds o... per ce... doesn'... has the help of an exp...

• Despite millions lars in advertising ar ing life insurance families are under The biggest selling are for $5,000 an enough to support for about a year. With the help of

P HART

Experts: Few Get Money's Worth i...

Monday, October 10,

More

WASHINGTON—Some shrill, traditional critics of t... ance industry leave the impres... agents are crooks and that o... ...rance which usually inve...

...ife Insurance

By Jean Carper
Washington Post Service

...shington, D.C. — They say they're ...orried. The life insurance industry, ...all, is one of the most formidable ... of private enterprise, with $320 ... in assets.

... companies buy and sell real estate ...as the Empire State Building as cas-...as the rest of us buy toothpaste. ... put billions into housing projects, ...ing centers, banks and Wall Street, ...rough their investments help shape ...ructure of society.

...ce the late 1800s they have been a ... economic force in the country, vir-... unaccountable to anyone and cer-...not to Uncle Sam.

...w all of that may be changing he-... of a new spurt of fed... insurance, including a ...y the Federal Trade Cor... industry is trying hard ...nce of a threat, but its a... ...m and bravado. When a ...TC's investigations, Rot... f the American Council ...ce, the companies' trad... said, "They would be dar... knew what they were doin"

Council Moves

I, in September the counc. w York office and staff o ...ington. Why? Waldron adn ...s to be closer to the action, ...end off the growing intru ...Sam.

... federal assault is coming ...al directions. Last January a ...Justice Department asked ... the antitrust immunity Co ...nsurance companies in 1945 ...cCarran-Ferguson Act. (Tha ...mmunizes insurance compa ...st federal controls in matter. ...regulated by the states.)

. Edward W. Brooke (R-Mass. ...ntroduced a bill the industry fo ...open the door wide to federal ...n. Brooke's bill, among otl ...would allow federal chartering ...as state chartering of insuran ...nies and would create a three pe ...deral Insurance Commission.

... Securities and Exchange Commis. ...taking a closer look at the annuity ...f life insurance with an eye toward ...r regulation. And last year the FTC ...an investigation into life insurance ...practices

That hardly seem ...tion in a free enter industry long shie... it could be a bomt

Such respecte... Moorhead, a ret Belth, a life insura... ana University, agree tha... disclosure could have severe rep... sions and send some companies out o business.

Moorhead says: "I don't think that's necessarily bad; there are too many companies now."

Test Going On

Nor is the FTC naive about the i... The proposal is delibe... bring ...

TV Listings on Page 6

THE MILWAUK...

—Classified Ads Start on Page 8

Life Insurance Firms...

the t... would require ...in states where the ...tion, to give consu... so ...

The Star-Ledger

Newark, N.J. Monday, April 17, 1978

The Newspaper for New Jersey

an industry survey calle ..., " which showed half o ...g a decline in living ...ncluded that ...ciy l..

Federal Inve...

Press Life In...

GAUGING ADEQUACY OF STATE RULES

FTC scrutinizing life insurance

By HERB JAFFE

The Federal Trade Commission (FTC) has launched an investigation into life insurance costs and selling practices based on a strong concern that consumers are not being adequately protected by state regulations. The Star-Ledger has learned

Michael Lynch, FTC economist in Washington, confirmed that 110 life insurers are being sent lengthy questionnaires by the FTC to help determine how wide the range of costs are to the public for similar types of life policies.

The investigation is similar to those already announced by a congressional committee and under consideration by a U.S. Senate committee into selling and cost practices involving health insur-... and ... ...n...

Lynch, who is heading the investigation, called it "the first effort by the FTC into life insurance practices. Basically, we are involved in a life insurance disclosure investigation."

He explained that the U.S. Senate antitrust and monopoly subcommittee in 1972 gathered "considerable information during hearings on the tremendous range of costs between similar life insurance policies. We are taking that data and comparing it to the figures for 1977 ..see if anything has been done to improve things for life insurance consum...ers"

One purpose of the study, Lynch explained, is to develop a program of cost disclosure which may ultimately be recommended to Congress.

One of our alternatives might be to ...ulation over life

that state regulation in life insuranc so weak it "could be resulting in v spread deceptions by certain co... nies "

The investigation is being con... ed in conjunction with Purdue Un... ty, Lynch said, adding that FTC r... sentatives already had visited state insurance departments, inc New Jersey

"At present, New Jersey is u life insurance cost disclosure ... that was adopted as a model NAIC (National Association of In Commissioners), and which we an awful system In fact, Nev was one of the first to adopt th last January." he said

Lynch explained that the p life insurance is that the avera does not know what kind of pol

(Please turn to Page 12

Firms on Ov...

Hidden Cost...

INSURANCE, From Page C1

Moorhead says: "I don't think that's necessaril are too many companies now." Nor is the FTC the impact. Its effort is deliberately designed to major reforms in the industry. Asked if the FTC would make companies shape up or fold. Mi... chief economist for the investigation, says: "I ce so "

Conducting the investigation for the FTC is a of economists and lawyers who must proceed cause of the McCarran-Ferguson Act. On the the industry, which, despite its outward displa ual interest in the FTC inquiry

22-A—THE DETROIT NEWS—Wednesday, February 21, 1973

Nader urges law to protect consumer

Life insurance firms und...

revealed previously secret actuarial inform... thing. Hart, using a cost analysis system de... found that the actual cost of "whole life" i...

Excerpts from the *Trend Report:* The Impact of Inflation on Life Insurance Companies and Their Policyholders

"Our business is on a self-destruct course if it continues its present emphasis on individual, whole-life products," the actuaries, economists, vice-presidents, investors, and administrators of America's leading life insurance companies and trade associations warned their bosses in 1974. In a report by the Institute of Life Insurance (since 1974, merged into the monolithic trade association, the American Council of Life Insurance, based in Washington, D.C.) entitled "Life Insurance Companies and the Impact of Inflation," the leadership of the cash-value whole-life insurance industry took a hard look at their practice of selling such policies during inflationary times, and concluded that someone—either the companies or their policyholders—was going to have to dig deep into his pocket in order to keep the traditional cash-value life insurance industry financially solvent.

Known as the *1974 Trend Report,* it was issued only to top executives of insurance companies, not to the public or the hapless insurance agents. The conclusions arrived at by four of the leading life insurance economists—Kenneth M. Wright of the American Life Insurance Association, Mona G. Coogan of Metropolitan Life, J. Robert Ferrari of Prudential, and Francis H. Schott of the Equitable Life Assurance Society—were definitely not the sort that would strike confidence into the public mind, if they became generally known.

The economists projected the future of the whole-life insurance game under three different possible rates of inflation between 1974 and 1990. They called these projections or predictions "Scenarios I, II, and III." Two of the possibilities (Scenarios II and III) were so unlikely that the *Trend Report* scarcely mentions them: (a) a steady rate of inflation at

4.5 percent from 1974 into the future, or (b) massive social upheaval that causes inflation to drop from 12 percent in 1977 to *zero* in 1978, gradually increasing to 2½ percent by 1990. The *Trend Report* and most independent economists would agree that the most likely course for inflation to follow can be seen in the graph labeled Scenario I, a steady fluctuation in its rate from 6 percent to 10 percent to 8 percent to 12 percent to 10 percent, ending up near 15 percent annually by 1990.

With the value of money eroding so rapidly, how can the life insurance industry continue to promote cash-value life insurance and persuade anyone to "save" their cash values in this way? The picture looked grim to the whole-life companies as you can see on the chart below. And what remedy did the *Trend Report* offer?

"Scenarios I and II suggested that the business might seek such options as a floating or indexed rate for policy loans, or even a release from the obligation of guaranteed cash values."

So the companies and executives may back away from the guaranteed cash values on which they've built their fortunes. We will see, as we go

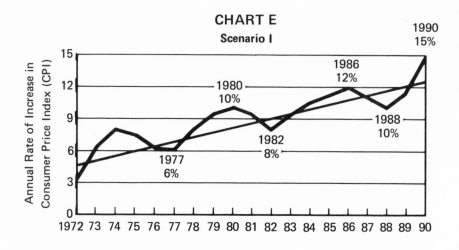

(Note: Since the rate of increase of inflation is never zero, the dips in the graph—Chart E—indicate lower rates of price increases—*not lower prices*.)

through this report, that the companies will be moving away from many guarantees they used to feed to prospective clients. A common sales pitch agents use on customers is "Guaranteed cash-value life insurance is the greatest savings plan ever conceived by the mind of man!" Now that it might not be in the best interests of the companies—never mind the consumers' interests—it suddenly isn't such a great idea.

"Traditional cash-value life insurance will not provide as much purchasing power for beneficiaries, even though policyholders add to their coverage. Premiums for increased coverage can presumably be afforded by inflated salaries, but what is often overlooked in this presumption is that wage increases lead to higher taxes, diminishing the ability of policyholders to 'afford' additional insurance. The purchasing power of permanent life insurance will be impaired. Company operating expenses will be higher, including sales expenses."

The economists know what's going on, even if agents and consumers don't. Agents commonly argue that you need *more* "traditional cash-value life insurance" because of inflation. In this report, the life insurance industry punctures that myth in its own evaluation of the effect of inflation on the purchasing power and sales of so-called permanent (whole-life) products. All the same, agents have continued to sell people yet another permanent "piece of the Rock" as a supposed hedge against inflation, even though Prudential's chief economist, J. Robert Ferrari, was one of the participants in the *Trend Report*.

"The public's perception of the situation will be important. People will not be unaware of the drastic impact of inflation on fixed-dollar amounts over long periods, a situation that will be repeatedly stressed in consumer-oriented publications.

"These conditions suggest the likelihood of a major shift away from traditional cash-value life insurance with its fixed-dollar savings element, toward various forms of term insurance. The cost effectiveness of term insurance may not be impaired as much because it is primarily a current-dollar operation. However, term insurance generates little investment yield to offset inflating expenses. Also, term insurance may have to be higher priced to provide the agent with compensation lost as a result of diminished whole-life sales. The conditions would be good for a shift toward greater reliance on group term and, particularly among the mass market, toward reliance on Social Security."

So the prices of term insurance may very well be raised (some already have been) in order to subsidize the whole-life companies and their sales forces. The price of protection will go up, but who is protecting whom?

"There could be a massive drain on individual life insurance reserves and the underlying investments. Even if policies are not cashed in,

137

policy loans may be used more heavily than ever before. (Though the salaries of many people may keep up with inflation, consumers will not necessarily see it that way, and may instead feel extra pressure on their personal budgets.) Policy loans can be used to finance additional coverage or to pay premiums on existing coverage. Or they can be used simply to supplement available funds for general family purposes. When interest rates are high, policy loans will be preferred over other sources of credit."

Are you one of the people who agreed to have your loan rate raised in your policy from 6 to 8 percent, in hopes of getting higher dividends later? Read on:

"Therefore, mutual companies might review dividend policy. This could include a new look at the investment-year method, the possibility of a level rather than an increasing dividend flow, and possible reduction of terminal dividends to recognize the market-value loss due to withdrawal of funds when asset values are depressed on a current yield basis. A further point: if there is real danger of a major drain on life insurance reserves that would threaten solvency, perhaps we should start reducing dividends now to build up additional surplus."

So the companies can be doubly covered, by having raised the loan rates and by reserving the right to cut back on dividends simultaneously. True double jeopardy for the policyholder. Especially vulnerable are the longtime policyholders at the Equitable Life Assurance Society (one of the participants in preparing this report) which has changed to the "investment-year" method for calculating dividends. "New" policyholders get a break at the expense of these older policyholders.

"Companies issuing non-participating products [those not paying dividends] will be affected sooner than companies issuing participating products [those paying dividends] since the latter would be able to offset increasing expenses by decreasing dividends. However, if as anticipated, dividend increases fall short of policy holder and purchaser expectations, these companies, too, would experience severe problems."

Translation: The mutual companies believe that since they have more fat in their budgets, they can last longer than non-participating companies, even those which may be more efficiently run than mutuals. But they can't escape the crunch of inflation; and the "severe problems" that they, the mutuals, would experience would mean a loss of business.

The *Trend Report* continues by pointing out that *in the future* the rate of inflation rather than changes in the family will be the determining factor as to what type of insurance people will need. The report exhorts the insurance executives to consider "the relationship of our product to the consumer's changing needs due to inflation." Yet, cash-value life insurance sales as well as inflation have been dramatically escalating every year since 1974. Obviously, the insurance executives promoting cash-

138

value life insurance have paid no attention to their own top economists, actuaries, investment officers, administrators, and marketing and products officers.

Because of the increasing inflation rate, the report suggests that automatically increasing the coverage on the policy, within certain limits, would be a good idea for the consumer; but it also recognizes that "the agent frequently objects to automatic increases in coverage" because these give him no chance to collect another commission from his client. "We wonder if that psychology can be permitted to predominate in the future," muses the report.

"To the extent that life insurance as we now know it diminishes in the future, particularly the permanent type of plans and individual sales, the business might want to consider converting life insurance to some other type of insurance at the older ages and later years of the policy. Conceivably this could involve conversion to health insurance, some type of retirement benefits, or casualty and property insurance. This would address the consumer's needs from the point of view of total risk management and may be something both desirable and necessary for the life insurance industry to consider."

So rather than giving you your cash values and dividends when they mature, the industry would prefer to keep that money and give you more insurance. This not only speaks eloquently of the greed of the companies and their presumption in deciding what type of insurance you need, but demolishes the hackneyed argument of agents that "you need *permanent* insurance!" Just when you could get your money back, the agent would inform you that what you *really* need now is property or health insurance. And why is this plan "both desirable and necessary for the life insurance industry?" It is obviously desirable, from their point of view, to keep your money; but is their business so shaky that it is also necessary?

"It is likely that increasing inflation will have a detrimental effect on the persistency of our business. This would apply to the business already in force and should be kept in mind in the products we might design for the future."

The reader might take his cue from this prediction, and transfer his insurance from a whole-life company to a term company that will weather the inflationary storm.

"There is the possibility that the life insurance business would want to consider a product which has premium rates that are guaranteed only for a certain period of time, such as 10, 5, or even 1 year, and which are then subject to increase, on a class basis, within certain predetermined limits. This may become necessary to consider as inflation affects the insurance business on the costs of the service and benefits it contractually guarantees for many decades into the future . . . and as the premium for

139

the life insurance policy initially paid is made as low as possible in order to appeal to the consumer, who is crunched by the effects of inflation on his checkbook."

Since the companies are here suggesting that they will retain the option to raise your premium rates after "10, 5, or even 1" year, this is one more good argument for buying insurance now that has guaranteed rates to age 100. You can get annual renewable term insurance with this feature.

In order to keep your cash in their coffers, the companies are urged to consider this novel idea: "One further suggestion: pay benefits in goods and services rather than dollars."

How bizarre! Will beneficiaries be paid in potatoes and shoeshines? In Cadillacs and hot waxes? Will the agent bring over a bag of groceries and make you breakfast each day? We don't know, but we wish we did.

The *Trend Report* admits that reforms are going to come to the industry, whether it likes it or not. Inflationary pressures will succeed where legislation has failed in forcing companies to sell term insurance and to let go of captive agents.

> As a result, life insurance companies may have to concentrate on selling those forms of insurance with a short-term "term" element—e.g., term life insurance, property insurance, casualty insurance [such as auto liability], personal and professional liability, etc.
>
> If the life insurance business lost these higher premium elements from its product portfolio, it would then have a difficult time in maintaining an agency force such as exists today. We may also find insurance companies attempting to broaden their bases of operations by expanding into other lines: life and health companies into property and casualty, and vice versa.
>
> Although the ramifications of these developments were not fully explored, it seems evident that they could result in the demise of small and medium-size companies—and the greater dominance of the relatively large, multiple-line companies.
>
> Both Scenarios I and III would appear to involve another likely development: the encroachment of the Federal government so as to supply more of the insurance needs of the public. As a result, the life insurance business would be faced with a steadily decreasing market. The consensus was that the remaining market would, to a greater extent than is the case today, be served by group and mass-merchandising techniques, and be further confined to higher-income groups.

You can almost imagine the authors of the *Trend Report* spitting that word "term" out of the corners of their mouths. Insurance executives and most agents dread selling the stuff. As most of them are quick enough to point out, there are not enough profits or commissions in term insurance. In addition, they will loudly bellow that life insurance has to be "sold," and who is going to do all that "prospecting" to find sales if agents aren't paid enough commissions. Also note that the industry is resigned to ever increasing monopolization of the business as smaller companies fold, another classic perversion of free enterprise.

> Agent compensation being generally proportional to premium income, the commission system today pays some agents very handsomely. Others do not do well and there is high turnover in the first few years. Companies are spending increasing amounts to recruit and finance agents. Even without the pull of inflation, there have been attempts to improve training, support services, and segment markets to the point where the sales of life insurance do not depend only on the affluent veteran or the rookie selling to his family and friends. The pressure of inflation on costs has speeded up this process.
>
> If the commission system is retained, can the structure of commissions be correctly adjusted to the changes in product implied under Scenario I—most notably, a fairly large-scale abandonment of cash-value life insurance in favor of term products? How much more term would have to be sold with no increase in commission? How much would term commissions have to increase for agents selling term to equal their income under their present mix?
>
> This would vary for different companies. Some companies are already selling more term than permanent, so that a change would not be drastic. Others have already provided their sal force with a whole portfolio of term-type products. These companies appear to be in a better position to weather the inflationary storms.

This is an astonishing admission for the life insurance industry to make, even in this "secret" document—that the term insurance companies will be in a much better position to survive the inflation crisis. Obviously, the term insurance companies won't have to manipulate their policyholders by paying them in "goods and services," or by twisting their policies to health or homeowner coverage—one more good reason to buy term from a term company.

Perhaps the most frightening portion of the *Trend Report* is contained in a few terse words further along in the extract, which comments on the future of cash-value life insurance.

"Cash-value life insurance products— To the extent that such products could still be sold, short-term investments and policy loans would dominate over the next 15 years. The attempt would be to minimize losses on withdrawals, with a conscious effort to restructure assets as much as possible. Pressures may mount for some kind of moratorium on policy loans."

"Some kind of moratorium on policy loans." That phrase doesn't mean much to the casual reader unless he is familiar with the last moratorium on cash-value policy loans, which happened in 1933, during the grip of the Great Depression. At that time, millions of Americans were ruined and needed any money they could get their hands on. For many, this meant borrowing the cash values out of their insurance policies or canceling them. The policyholders were under the delusion, fostered by their local friendly insurance agent, that this was their money in an account owned by them.

Well, so many millions of people demanded their cash values back that, between 1929 and 1936, 14 percent of all the life insurance companies involved in cash-value banking and investment went into receivership. The Depression was still deepening, and the major companies knew they would be the next to fold. Curiously enough, not one company went under because of its straight insurance business. Those that failed went on the rocks as a result of their banking and investment activities.

Enough was enough. Banks were closing, and more and more people were turning to the insurance companies to borrow their cash values or cancel their policies. In February of 1933, a secret meeting of executives from the large Eastern insurance companies was held in New York. Also present were many other executives from smaller companies, and the insurance commissioners from nineteen states. The companies tried naked power on the commissioners, telling them if they were required to honor their cash-value loans and accept all cancellations they would go broke; they'd have to dump all their assets on the open market, which would absolutely sink the American economy.

One executive offered a resolution requesting that the state insurance commissioners declare a moratorium on cash-value demands and policy loans. It was a big hit with the insurance companies, passing with only one dissenting vote.

The insurance commissioners balked, aware that the move was, at that time, completely illegal. The insurance companies were saved when a bank holiday was declared, closing those financial institutions. The insurance executives explained to the commissioners that since they acted

142

as banks, they should be allowed the same sort of holiday. On March 1, 1933, the first life insurance moratorium went into effect.

Unlike the banks, the insurance companies didn't close completely. They continued to accept new policies, and they demanded that their policyholders continue to make their payments on premiums; they only ceased issuing policy loans and stopped honoring canceled policies with a demand for cash values back. In fact, since people couldn't get money out of their banks, and couldn't get a loan to make their premium payments, they had to lapse their policies and lose their insurance protection. The surviving insurance companies grew fat off America's misery during the Depression.

It happened in 1933. It can happen again in the 1980s. There wouldn't be a bank moratorium this time to legitimize the insurance moratorium, since banks are now insured by the Federal Deposit Insurance Corporation. But the insurance companies are considering the possibility of a moratorium anyway. By threatening to sell their government bonds and their interests in major American corporations, the insurance companies could easily bully the U.S. government into allowing them another moratorium—as they did in 1933.

The *Trend Report* doesn't comment on the social chaos a moratorium would create, nor on its effects on the average individual policyholder. What does worry the Institute of Life Insurance is whether, in the midst of all this, with America falling apart, their companies will be threatening a virtual coup d'état if their moratorium isn't approved? The *Trend Report* dwells on the horrible prospect that top executives may have to accept smaller offices:

"Offices may become less prestigious—smaller and with fewer frills. (However, an alternative possibility is that if executive salaries are not keeping pace with living costs, it may become more necessary to retain these kinds of status symbols to keep up morale.)"

The possibility of providing large offices as a "dividend" is kept open, just so these insurance company executives won't have to suffer complete humiliation. There is also the possibility that the executives reading this report would outrightly reject any suggestion that they might have to tighten their own belts.

The economists and other top company and trade association executives who prepared this *Trend Report* surely had no intention of being sarcastic, but one can't help but laugh at the mistitling of the last suggestion on the corporate belt-tightening list.

Many of the company's non-monetary benefits, such as free or subsidized lunches and recreational facilities, will undoubtedly be reduced, because the money will be needed to pay salaries.

B. Work Hours:

The current pressures to reduce work hours will abate, because of the need for greater productivity to offset the effect of continually rising inflation.

C. Corporate Social Responsibility:

Many projects currently being undertaken by companies in the area of corporate social responsibility will be more carefully tested against the long-term health and safety of the company. The overall issue facing the companies will be survival, with some marginal companies not making it through to the end of the scenario period. The main responsibility of the company will be to continue to exist, rather than to divert attention to other needs of society.

There's corporate social responsibility for you. The bottom line (did you ever doubt it) is the financial survival of the company and its executives. The policyholders can fend for themselves.

The conclusions of the report are worth quoting in their entirety:

In Conclusion

While it is difficult to summarize the wide-ranging thoughts that surfaced from these meetings, several general conclusions emerged which were consistent among the economists, investment officers administrators and marketing and products officers.

First and of greatest import was the conviction that under any of the three scenarios, especially Scenarios I and III, the life insurance business would face real danger. For example, while all the participants were able to talk about specific ways the business could operate under Scenario I, the overriding sentiment was that *the society and the business would be on a self-destruct course that could not be manageable* for as long a time as the scenario represented. Solvency would be threatened, and operating costs would be unpredictable. The demand for our products would undergo severe blows on several counts: governmental security systems would swell, inflation and taxes would bite significantly into disposable income, and fixed-dollar savings and investment vehicles would lose their appeal. Therefore, specific points raised in this report notwithstanding, the overall patterns depicted in at least two of the scenarios are gloomy, if not downright disastrous.

The second overall conclusion was that the social and political considerations implied in or resulting from these scenarios would have secondary and tertiary impacts on our business which could have at least as much, if not more, effect on our stability as would the primary implications of inflation itself. For example, Scenarios II and III could easily lead to strict governmental restrictions and regulations imposed on investments, products, and operating procedures that could dampen any innovative or expansive efforts to offset the inflationary environment.

Both of the above conclusions paint such a dismal picture that the conference participants were led inevitably to a third and critical overall judgment—*the life insurance business must deploy whatever means it has within its power to avoid either long-range patterns of volatile inflation or the necessity for severe controls* which short-range extreme fluctuations would require. The sum of opinion was that all these scenarios, in containing various seeds of destruction of our conventional patterns of business, necessitate the asking of some questions basic to the business's survival:

In the event of continuing inflation, are we prepared to make radical changes in our ways of doing business? and

What can we realistically do to support every plausible effort to bring inflation under control?

The overall consensus was that the business *must* face the challenge posed by inflation and deal with it now. This brings us full circle to the Introduction of this report, in which it is stated that this project was designed as one first step in helping the business build toward further discussion and action.

The major insurance companies, especially the so-called policyholder-controlled giant mutuals, have laid matters on the line. They are on a destruction course, doomed by their own greed. The open question is whether you will go down with them, or instead of them—or whether you will make a *commitment* to put your insurance money where it will be relatively safe and will give you true protection.

The Million Dollar Round Table

The most successful agents are sitting about the Million Dollar Round Table. The Million Dollar Round Table is the Holy Grail of the life insurance agent, headquartered in the Camelot of the Midwest, Chicago. The organization is set up to encourage agents to write $1.25 million each in life insurance annually, which might not be so bad except that when they calculate how much insurance has been sold, whole-life counts for more than term insurance. Whole-life policies with mutual companies count the most, followed by whole-life with stock companies, with term insurance bringing up the rear. Just so that agents get the point, Section 20.5 of the constitution of the group deals specifically with how they can get extra points by converting term policies to whole-life.

The success that agents have in persuading people to convert term policies to whole-life insurance has been documented by Arthur L. Williams, associate professor of insurance and real estate at Pennsylvania State University. After studying more than 20,000 term policies, Williams found that 90 percent of all policies were terminated or converted—45 percent of them within the first year, 72 percent by the second year. Less than one policy in ten survived the period it was written for, Williams found. This is a shining testimonial to the vigor of whole-life agents who sally forth to convert term to whole-life insurance. Naturally, these lapse rates are expensive for the insurance companies, so they raise their premiums to make up for it.

The Million Dollar Round Table represents the cream of the crop, from the insurance companies' viewpoint, because any agent who takes this system seriously will be out there selling the most expensive policies he can to his customers, regardless of their financial needs. Yet in the Code of Ethics of the National Association of Life Underwriters, which the Million Dollar Round Tablers swear by, they pledge to "keep the needs of my clients always uppermost," and "to present accurately,

honestly, and completely every fact essential to my client's decisions."
Obviously, it is impossible for an agent to hold to those pledges and sit
at the Million Dollar Round Table at the same time. Is your agent a
member of the M.D.R.T.—or has he been replaced by a "new" Abernathy?

APPENDIX C

Excerpts from the *Hart Hearings*

On February 20 through 23, 1973, and on July 16, 1974, the United States Senate Subcommittee on Antitrust and Monopoly, chaired by the late Senator Philip A. Hart, considered the practices of the life insurance industry. They invited speakers from both inside and outside the business to speak, critics and supporters of the life insurance industry. Some of the evidence and testimony presented to Senator Hart's committee was so shocking that the senator felt compelled to draft a bill that would have cleaned up the practices of companies and agents. Some of the most powerful evidence is presented here.

A veritable parade of consumer advocates appeared at the Hart committee hearings to call for regulation of the insurance business in one form or another. Ralph Nader stated that the insurance industry's "contrived complexity, secrecy, and public relations have fulfilled a strongly supplementary camouflage function. Hidden behind this camouflage are two principal levers of maximizing life insurance company profit or surplus—deception and, ironically, gross waste. Neither redounds in any way to the consumer's benefit. For almost seventy years, the life insurance industry has been a smug sacred cow feeding the public a steady line of sacred bull." Nader merely had to quote from the "Widow's Study" (Women Be Wise, p. 116) to prove his contention that the industry had failed to provide protection for the supposed beneficiaries of insurance —widows and their children.

Professor Joseph M. Belth of Indiana University—who has long been hated by the insurance industry for insisting that they include the interest lost on cash values in their estimates of the annual cost of a policy and break down the premium of a whole-life policy to show plainly the actual amount of death protection and savings—summed up the situation this way:

The market for individual life insurance in the United States is characterized by ignorance, complexity, and apathy. Buyers are ignorant about the amount of life insurance they need, about the kinds of policies that are appropriate for them, and about the large price difference among life insurance companies. Many life insurance agents are also ignorant of these things, because state licensing examinations generally require only a minimum of knowledge, and because most company and industry training programs place the emphasis on sales techniques rather than technical knowledge. . . .

Buyers are apathetic about life insurance because it is associated with the unpleasant subject of death. Most life insurance, therefore, is bought because a life insurance agent persuades the buyer to take action rather than procrastinate. To overcome the apathy of buyers, agents must be highly trained in the techniques of salesmanship. The necessity for this type of training leads to the frequent omission of adequate technical training, and to the development of a wide variety of deceptive sales practices.

Then Professor Belth reaffirmed his belief that strong "truth-in-life-insurance laws are necessary to correct the situation which now exists."

Although most people don't understand insurance policies when they buy them, they realize a few things within a year or two afterward. First, many people question their need for the policy, and they wonder if the policy they bought is really suitable for their family's needs, especially if they can't keep up the premium payments. The client might then cancel the policy and become part of the statistics on "lapse rates." In the business, dropping your policy is known as letting it "lapse."

Some companies' policies are so short-lived that they should sell life insurance on their life insurance policies. Dean Sharp, who was Senator Hart's chief investigator and legal counsel on life insurance abuses for eleven years, summed up the high lapse rates of major insurance companies in a 1975 report for the Smith-Barney research organization of Washington, D.C.:

The subcommittee's survey lapse data shows that an *average* 18 percent of non-debit-system straight-life policies [that is, the usual whole-life policy] issued by 59 large companies to men aged 35 lapsed at the end of the first year. Other lapse data collected by the subcommittee for the biggest-selling policy of 138 non-debit companies submitting data, shows that 55 had 13-month lapse rates (as measured by number of policies) of 25 percent or more. And, eleven non-debit companies had 13-month lapse rates in excess of 40 percent for their top selling policy.

The subcommittee lapse data for the 59 large companies shows also that a cumulative average of 47 percent of the original group of 35-year-old men lapsed at the end of the tenth year. So, by the relative early age of 45, when family financial responsibilities are fairly burdensome, only 53 percent of the husbands or heads of households retained their cash-value policies. The 10-year cumulative range for the mutual companies was from 21 percent for Northwestern Mutual to 52 percent for John Hancock. The 10-year cumulative range for stock companies was from 29 percent for Southwestern Life to 66 percent for Fidelity Union Life.

Dr. Belth continually presses the point that "many life insurance sales presentations are characterized by either the absence of reliable price information or the presence of deceptive price information. For example, there may be a reference to premiums of cash-value policies, but such information is not a reliable indicator of the price of the protection: And when the elements of the price structure are discussed in greater detail in the interview, the potential for deception is high."

As Senator Hart comments with reference to high early lapse rates: "Perhaps they [consumers] were overwhelmed with figures in such a way that they were confused about the cost and benefits of what they bought."

According to the Senator, high early lapse rates also may mean: "Consumers may be buying what they don't need or can't afford because they don't understand."

This lack of understanding may be particularly important in explaining the unusually high purchase *and* lapse rates among the young. Fifty percent of all ordinary policies were sold to people between the ages of 15 through 29, the life insurance industry found. Only one policy in four was bought by people aged 35 and over. The young are particularly vulnerable to the pitch of the agent, the industry found. Ninety percent of the young are concerned about their future financial security, and only 8 percent said that saving money "is not really necessary." The young were also found to have especially high lapse rates.

Some individual companies and policies deserve special mention for their astonishingly high lapse rates in the thirteenth month of the policy, as indicated in the Hart subcommittee's 1974 hearings. (The thirteenth month is when policies are renewed for the first time, or dropped.) Allstate's modified endowment lapsed at the rate of 52.2 percent in the thirteenth month. Banker's Life & Casualty's 20-pay life "with special options" lost 44.9 percent of its buyers at the first annual renewal. Standard Life Insurance Company of Indiana's ordinary-life product lapsed at a rate of 45.5 percent by the thirteenth month. United Insurance Company of America's ordinary life "paid-up-at-96" policy lost 56 percent of its buyers! These figures are high, but not unusually so. Many other companies' policies come close to these lapse rates. And these are all picked from the *three best-selling policies* of the respective companies, so these lapse rates are widespread in America.

The big mutual insurance companies are the most costly to the consumer. Senator Hart's subcommittee, found that in 1972 the cost in lost premiums mounted into the millions of dollars due to early lapses. John Hancock's policyholders lost $4.9 million, Prudential's lost $6.4 million, Metropolitan's lost $9.7 million, Equitable's lost $6.6 million, New York Life's lost $9.2 million, and Mutual of New York's (MONY's) lost $4.1 million in dropped policies. These, remember, are figures for only a few companies, for only one year, and are only due to lapses in the first year.* By multiplying these out by the hundreds of life insurance companies in America, and by figuring that this has been going on for more than a century, you can begin to grasp the dimensions of the waste that companies, their agents, and their policyholders suffer. And all by selling certain kinds of policies that their customers didn't really need or want. The companies don't make any money in the first year, as it takes about three to seven years for the company to begin making profit. The agent doesn't make the commissions on renewals that he needs, and ultimately this waste reduces the "dividends" that mutual policyholders hope to get back from the mutuals.

Washington, D.C., attorney Richard Phillips, a student and critic of the industry, commented for the Washington *Post*, "These new lapse-rate figures cut the ground out from under the industry argument" that only whole-life insurance provides needed protection at older ages. "If less than a third of insurance buyers continue their policies into their old age, is the need for death protection in those later years as widespread or great as the industry would have people believe? And if companies like Equitable fully expect a fourth of their customers to drop their so-called 'permanent' insurance after just a year, how 'permanent' is it?"

* The FTC staff, using the Hart subcommittee data, "have estimated aggregate consumer losses due to first-year lapsation (i.e., thirteenth month) to be in excess of 200 million dollars a year."

As Dean Sharp commented, "If any other industry found a quarter to half of the public rejected its supposedly 'lifetime' products within a few months or a year, it would begin to wonder whether it was selling the right product. But not the life insurance industry. It keeps on force-feeding the public the same products in the same way, in spite of these tremendous dropout rates."

The life insurance companies have discovered that the poor can produce unexpected windfall profits. The poor may not have much money individually, but there are *so many* of them, and they are generally so uninformed that they make easy marks for slick agents, if the agents can develop a route like a milkman so he can milk a whole poor neighborhood of their butter-and-egg money for whole-life premiums. Agents make personal visits weekly or monthly to collect premiums. Economic discrimination is practiced upon the poor in an unusually cruel way. The poor are nearly always offered whole-life policies, almost never term, and even these policies are offered only at grossly inflated rates. According to Philip Stern of the Washington *Post*, on June 8, 1975, the poor are often misled into buying whole-life insurance at rates 300 to 500 percent higher than middle-class buyers. Naturally, they can afford only policies offering a death benefit of $500 to $2500. If the life insurance companies offered these people term insurance, they could afford a reasonable death benefit. The companies do not make the offer, however.*

One reason the cost per $1000 of insurance is so high is the great amount of profits companies make from this type of insurance. Again, according to the 1975 Philip Stern article in the Washington *Post*, reprinted a month later in the *Congressional Record*, Life of Virginia made, in 1973, only 16.1 percent profit on its ordinary life (the type most sold to middle class on up) policies, but squeezed 51.6 percent out of its "industrial" policies (those sold to low-income customers). Similarly, Monumental made 16.5 percent on ordinary life and 42.1 percent on the "industrial" life—a monumental boost to their profits. Home Security made 9.3 percent on ordinary life and 26.5 percent on their industrial life policies.

The corporate giants are just as morally bankrupt. John Hancock and the Combined Insurance Company of Chicago, the biggest "monthly-debit" insurers, sold 400,000 policies in 1971. Not a single one was term insurance. Prudential did slightly better; just 99.7 percent of its monthly-debit policies were whole life; the remaining three-tenths of 1 percent were term.

Getting the facts on the huge price difference between policies to the public was a pet project of former Pennsylvania Insurance Commissioner

* The authors found an exception. The American Republic Insurance Companies of Des Moines, Iowa and New York City specialize in offering a reasonably priced, decreasing term policy for those markets served by the whole-life debit companies.

Herbert Denenberg, the biggest burr under the saddle that the insurance companies have ever had. Denenberg, while insurance commissioner, published a guide to insurance companies and their policies which pointed out the "cheapest and the dearest," as he put it. Denenberg circulated over 2 million copies of *The Shopper's Guide to Life Insurance* nationwide, causing some of the most expensive companies to lower the cost of their policies.

Denenberg also rejected the idea that insurance policies must necessarily be so complicated as to be almost unreadable. Using a test developed by Rudolph Flesch to measure the readability of material, Denenberg found that *Time* magazine, the textbook *Economics: Principles and Applications* by Paul Samuelson, and the *Wall Street Journal* were all easier to read than a Northwestern Mutual Life policy of the H.H. series. Blue Shield medical insurance policies were even harder to read, but *The Meaning of Relativity* by Albert Einstein, while very difficult, was far easier to understand than the standard automobile insurance policy.

Denenberg got Blue Shield to rewrite its medical policies so that they were almost as readable as the *Wall Street Journal,* a considerable improvement. He hoped to prod other insurance companies into following suit and making their policies more readable, but had little success.

Denenberg also pointed out the legislative clout of the industry when he commented that "if you review the history of insurance legislation in the United States, you will find that the regulatory laws have been written by the insurance industry."

Denenberg's views on cash-surrender-value life insurance are forthright: "Congress should pass a law making cash-value life insurance illegal, unless the insurance industry comes up with an adequate program of price disclosure designed to eliminate many of the abuses now made possible by public misunderstanding of this product." Abuses occur, according to Denenberg, because "40 percent of the agents are incompetent, and 80 percent of the insurers [that is, companies] are suspect." Denenberg elaborated on those figures when questioned by subcommittee staff counsel Dean Sharp, suggesting that they were conservative estimates.

Senator Hart's subcommittee also checked into just how valuable the "investment" portions of whole-life policies really are and, not surprisingly, found that a whole-life insurance policy is one of the poorest investments a person can make. Because of "front-end load" (the fact that the agent's commission and the cost of putting the policy on the books is taken out of the premiums paid in the first few years), the policy actually *loses* money as an investment for several years. As an example, after two years an Equitable policy has lost 80 percent of its value, a

Herbert Denenberg shows the motto of his insurance department to Senator Hart (*right*). Translated from the Latin, it reads: "The consumer has been screwed long enough."

Hancock policy 94 percent; MONY loses 92 percent, and Allstate and Travelers policies lose 100 percent of the premiums to expenses.

A policy must be maintained for about *ten years* before it even begins to show any real return for the client, and then it's nothing spectacular. Equitable returns 1.7 percent, Hancock .5 percent, MONY 1.8 percent, Allstate 5.1 percent, and Travelers 2.9 percent. This is better than an outright loss, as the first several years produce, but if the money had been put into a tax-deferred annuity, the policyholder would have gained about 7 percent *each year*.

Over the long run, the prospects for insurance policy investing are not good. Dean Sharp commented, "Even the most favorable rate of return for low-cost companies, like Massachusetts Mutual and Northwestern Mutual, rarely exceeds the 7 to 8 percent return that anyone can easily get, even on the smallest savings account. The overwhelming majority of the rates of return the subcommittee calculated were considerably below 5 percent."

Although it was never really in doubt, the subcommittee's research confirmed the chief criticism of whole-life insurance: that besides offering a smaller death benefit, its value as an investment is highly questionable, *particularly in inflationary times.*

Because the Subcommittee on Antitrust and Monopoly was concerned with consumer protection and abuses by the industry, it only lightly touched on another reason for regulation: infiltration of organized crime into the insurance industry.

Organized crime is one of the largest businesses in America, rivaling the insurance industry. Organized crime has made inroads into almost all legitimate business in order to invest its illegally gained money and get financing for shady projects. It should come as no surprise that organized crime also has its interests in the insurance industry; and although neither criminals nor insurance executives advertise the fact, the clues are there for anyone to ferret out.

For example, Aaron M. Kohn, managing director of the Metropolitan Crime Commission of New Orleans, addressed the convention of the National Association of Life Underwriters in 1970, and explained why insurance companies were so attractive to crime. Kohn said that criminals need financial institutions to hide illegal funds and to make loans to finance legal and illegal business; and when the criminals move in and take over a company, they gain ownership and control of the records and the funds of the company.

According to Kohn, "Insurance company funds [including your cash values] have helped capitalize Las Vegas gambling casinos"; the biggest numbers and gambling racketeer in Indianapolis bought an insurance company lock, stock, and barrel; labor bosses with underworld connections bargained with a company for group insurance, promising kickbacks to sweeten the pot; and a Louisiana criminal financier owns an insurance company doing interstate business, controls a bank with the local underworld boss's son on the board of directors, owns interest in four other insurance companies, and made moves to take over an insolvent insurer in Salt Lake City.

The National Association of Insurance Commissioners (NAIC) serves the insurance commissioners of the states by maintaining files and a library for them, and by researching various topics for them. The NAIC has what they call the "sharpshooter's file," a rogue's gallery of swindlers and gangsters whose stories are clipped from various newspapers and magazines. Although the file has much more information on swindlers than on organized crime, bits of the iceberg surface here and there.

The *Wall Street Journal* reported on September 20, 1973, that the Ford Motor Company managed to funnel executive expense money out of America to Bermuda by paying inflated premiums to a Bermuda-based insurance company, Transglobal Insurance Company. Ever wonder why your Ford cost more?

The Equity Funding Corporation of America was busted for inventing insurance policies out of thin air, and then selling them for cash to reinsurance companies. When auditors came to examine their books, teams of Equity employees worked late forging policy files and posing as policyholders to deceive the auditors.

In a private interview, an insurance company president confided that he heard that organized crime figures have raised money by having agents write large cash-value policies on gangsters, and then borrowing on the policies to raise money. The policyholder need not even exist; as long as an audit doesn't trip up the scheme, policies can be written on nonexistent people, and then others can show up to borrow the money from their cash values.

Even though the abuses by the insurance industry go back over a hundred years and are widespread enough to abuse almost every family in America, the insurance companies see no particular need for strong federal regulation. They feel that things are just fine the way they are, with fifty insurance commissioners in fifty states writing widely differing regulations to regulate companies on a state level. When the companies can't actually deny that reform is necessary, they argue that rushing into it is dangerous and all proposals require time to study them. On the surface, that may sound reasonable, but the industry has successfully put off any reform for over a century.

The industry has established numerous lobbying and research organizations to take the heat off them by stalling reform. The Conference of Insurance Legislators (COIL) is a good example. This group is essentially a front for the insurance industry which gets the good word out on insurance companies to legislators in many states. Too bad the consumer doesn't have such a pipeline straight to insurance legislators. COIL makes sure that the legislators know just what the industry wants in insurance regulation, and it gets it.

The National Association of Insurance Commissioners (NAIC) is a study and informational group that serves the state insurance commissioners. In eleven states the commissioners are elected; the rest are political appointees. NAIC's top staff man is Jon Hanson, a past assistant vice-president of the Northwestern Mutual Life Insurance Company of Milwaukee. Another influential member of NAIC is Robert E. Dineen, former superintendent of insurance of New York. Mr. Dineen came straight to his most influential NAIC consulting post from the presidency of Northwestern Mutual.

It might be fair to say at this point that perhaps there is too much influence from life insurance companies themselves on this association.

At any rate, at its convention on June 8, 1976, NAIC put out an interesting document detailing what they considered an appropriate insurance buyer's guide. This remarkable document fails to explain term insurance adequately, and, by its wording, seems to favor cash-value insurance, the industry's favorite product. It also fails to explain what a mutual company "dividend" really is. This is supposed to be the industry prototype of a Herb Denenberg–style buyer's guide to insurance! The insurance commissioners are supported by public funds. Doesn't the public deserve a better explanation of insurance than that?

There are myriad organizations binding together the insurance complex, of which COIL and NAIC are only two. While the years drag on, so do the studies of these groups. The industry apparently feels that as long as everybody's studying, no one's legislating or regulating them, so they're free to carry on their lucrative business.

The industry's position on federal regulation is clear-cut: they're against it. For example, the Pennsylvania Association of Life Underwriters recently asked a state court for an injunction to prevent that state's insurance commissioner, William Sheppard, from enforcing the new disclosure regulation that would require an agent to give a customer comparative cost information before closing the sale. The president of the organization stated that "Life underwriters, in theory, support the overall purpose of disclosing pertinent information. We believe our present position of supplying this information to our clients at the most opportune time for their understanding is our goal." When the "most opportune time" is, is left vague; but all too often the client or beneficiary never learns the truth.

Daniel L. Hurson, the chairman and president of the Acacia Mutual Life Insurance Company, wrote in the April 1976 issue of *Council Review:* "From the point of view of the chief executive, the most immediate element of this problem (the far-reaching problem of the cost of delivering our products to the buyers) is the prospect of some regulatory authority mandating 'disclosure' to such a degree that many companies caught in less attractive cost positions would have grave difficulties competing—perhaps even surviving—in the marketplace. If the most extreme advocates of price comparison at the point of sale were to have their way, this could become a real danger."

In other words, it's more important to protect the business of companies that overcharge than to let the consumer know how to get the best protection for his money. How candid!

The September 17, 1977, issue of *The National Underwriter,* the weekly magazine for insurance executives and agents, contained similarly warped views by Darrell Eichoff, the executive vice-president of Metropolitan Life. Eichoff warned his fellow executives that inflation was quickly eroding the life insurance business by rendering whole-life policies worthless. Predictably, he was concerned for the solvency of whole-life companies, not of their policyholders. Confronting the possibility that clients might switch to term insurance, he declared, "This might not be in the best interest of policyholders," and it "would seriously affect agents' earnings, as well as companies' cash flow positions." Just why policyholders should be so concerned about the companies' cash flow and the agents' earnings was not detailed by Eichoff. He did make some devastating comments that seemed to pertain to his own product, if one read between the lines: "Why would anyone sacrifice to purchase a life insurance policy today that will have little real dollar value 10 or 15 years from now? Why should anyone invest today in a pension that will be worth far less 20 years from now?" Why, indeed? the policyholder might well ask Mr. Eichoff.

Not all insurance executives are as callous to the needs of their policyholders as Eichoff and Hurson seem to be, however. Some are seeing the light, realizing that the public can't be fooled indefinitely, and they want to be in the vanguard of companies that can say they recognized the problem and acted on it before Congress forced them to. One is Michael H. Levy, founder of Standard Security Life Insurance Company of New York, now retired, who wrote in the August 1977 issue of *Insurance Marketing* magazine:

> Since 1945, I have been personally convinced that term insurance answers the needs of most buyers far more effectively than cash-value insurance does. Such was the case for 95 percent or more of the clients of my general brokerage operation. . . .
>
> With the growing sophistication of consumers and legislators, if agents continue to rationalize their sale of small amounts of insurance at high cost to their policyholders—and if chief executives of larger companies continue to brainwash their agents in favor of selling cash-value insurance—both agents and executives will find that they have rendered themselves, their companies and their industry a disservice.

This situation prompted Senator Hart to be "more convinced than ever that life insurance buyers need—and are not getting—clear, accurate, reliable, and adequate information about the cost and value of the policies they buy."

It was then that Dean Sharp began drafting a bill that would make certain disclosures mandatory—a "truth-in-life-insurance" bill more fully described in Appendix D, following.

Synopsis of Senate Bill 2065—Truth-in-Life-Insurance

By now it should be obvious that the greatest obstacle to matching up the right policy to the right client is lack of information—the kind of black-and-white, dollars-and-cents information insurance companies seem determined to withhold or at least befog with a lot of jargon. It is, in fact, just the sort of information the consumer *needs* to be able to make a decision about the right policy, and to keep from getting bilked.

To meet that need, Dean Sharp drafted Senate Bill 2065 for Senator Philip A. Hart. It died in the Committee on Commerce in 1975 because of insurance company lobbying and lack of legislative interest. Much was said about the bill creating a need for yet another big government bureaucracy. Such was not the case. Rather, it would have required the individual states to adopt regulations conforming to the provisions of Bill 2065. Table N is a synopsis of the information that an agent would have been required to give the consumer at the point of sale.

Here is a brief explanation of what each column in the chart would mean to you. Columns 7, 8, and 9 contain the information which the whole-life insurance companies would particularly like to conceal at the point of sale.

Column 1. Number of years (year by year) that the policy is kept in force.

Column 2. Comparable age for each policy year.

Column 3. Yearly premium cost.

Column 4. Amount of money the beneficiary would receive.

Column 5. The savings element—how much is refunded if the policy is canceled.

Column 6. Illustrated dividend. (This is not an estimate or a guarantee, but merely an illustration.)

Column 7. The actual amount of decreasing insurance protection as

Table M — Examples of Information on Life Insurance Policy Which Would Be Given Consumer at Point of Sale

[$25,000 participating straight life policy issued by Northwestern Mutual in 1973 to males aged 35]

Policy year (1)	Age at beginning of year (2)	Yearly premium (3)	Amount payable on death (4)	Amount payable on surrender (5)	Illustrated dividend (6)	Amount of protection (7)	Yearly price (8)	Yearly rate of return (percent) (9)
1	35	$578	$25,000	$ 0	$ 69	$25,000	$21.51	—
2	36	578	25,000	449	83	24,551	3.09	—
3	37	578	25,000	912	96	24,088	2.91	—
4	38	578	25,000	1,384	110	23,616	3.00	6.69
5	39	578	25,000	1,864	125	23,136	3.07	6.51
6	40	578	25,000	2,352	140	22,648	3.19	6.34
7	41	578	25,000	2,848	155	22,152	3.32	6.25
8	42	578	25,000	3,351	171	21,649	3.48	6.16
9	43	578	25,000	3,862	186	21,138	3.65	6.11
10	44	578	25,000	4,331	201	20,669	6.29	4.93
11	45	578	25,000	4,807	217	20,193	6.44	5.08
12	46	578	25,000	5,291	234	19,709	6.61	5.19
13	47	578	25,000	5,781	250	19,219	6.85	5.27
14	48	578	25,000	6,278	265	18,722	7.14	5.34
15	49	578	25,000	6,781	281	18,219	7.52	5.38
16	50	578	25,000	7,290	293	17,710	8.16	5.37
17	51	578	25,000	7,804	302	17,196	9.02	5.32
18	52	578	25,000	8,324	312	16,676	9.94	5.28
19	53	578	25,000	8,848	321	16,152	10.98	5.23
20	54	578	25,000	9,379	331	15,621	12.07	5.20
21	55	578	25,000	9,827	412	15,173	14.22	5.03
22	56	578	25,000	10,276	421	14,724	15.47	5.03
23	57	578	25,000	10,725	431	14,275	16.86	5.02
24	58	578	25,000	11,174	441	13,826	18.36	5.01
25	59	578	25,000	11,622	451	13,378	20.00	5.00
26	60	578	25,000	12,067	461	12,933	21.75	5.00
27	61	578	25,000	12,511	472	12,489	23.64	5.00
28	62	578	25,000	12,951	482	12,049	25.74	5.00
29	63	578	25,000	13,388	493	11,612	27.98	5.00
30	64	578	25,000	13,820	504	11,180	30.46	5.00
31	65	578	25,000	14,247	514	10,753	33.17	4.99
32	66	578	25,000	14,668	524	10,332	36.29	4.98
33	67	578	25,000	15,081	533	9,919	39.75	4.96
34	68	578	25,000	15,485	542	9,515	43.58	4.94
35	69	578	25,000	15,879	551	9,121	47.79	4.92
36	70	578	25,000	16,265	559	8,735	52.24	4.91
37	71	578	25,000	16,641	568	8,359	56.93	4.90
38	72	578	25,000	17,011	576	7,989	61.82	4.90
39	73	578	25,000	17,375	583	7,625	66.90	4.92
40	74	578	25,000	17,734	591	7,266	72.31	4.93

(Source: Congressional Record, July 8, 1975, page S11980)

it relates to increasing cash accumulation in column 5. (As you can see, this is how the insurance companies get you to provide your own protection with their "permanent" insurance.)

Column 8. This shows that the actual death protection *costs the insured more each year,* whether it be whole-life insurance or term insurance.

Column 9. The year-by-year rate of return assuming the dividend illustration figures become a reality.

In remarks made on the floor of the Senate on July 8, 1975, Senator Hart pointed out that his "truth-in-life-insurance" bill also contained provisions to protect the captive life insurance agent from his parent company:

> Because life insurance frequently has to be "sold," companies need agents, and the contractual relationships with agents tend to "lock in" an agent to one company. By this I refer to the general practice of requiring an agent to forfeit some of his commission if his contract terminates; most companies reserve the right to terminate an agent without cause. The irony is that the more business an agent produces for his company, the more he is "locked in" to that company.
>
> Because of the nature of an agent's contractual relationship with his company, he may be unable to do a really professional job for his client. For example, if his company sells an inferior or high-cost policy, the agent may be prevented from selling a competitor's superior or lower-cost policy, because of the fear of being terminated and forfeiting some of his commissions.
>
> In reality, the disclosure system in this bill will only reach its maximum effectiveness if agents are sufficiently independent so as to permit them to serve their clients in a truly professional manner. As one prominent casualty insurance company's advertisement in a national magazine asks:
>
> "How Objective Can an Insurance Agent Be If He Only Works for One Company?"
>
> This bill will allow agents to be sufficiently independent to do a truly professional job for the consumers.

APPENDIX E

Financial Planning Kit

The following Financial Kit is designed to help you determine the strong and weak points of your present financial situation. Once you understand the barriers to your future financial security, you can begin to solve the problems. Take the time to sit down with a financial planner, independent agent or broker, fill out the Financial Planning Questionnaire (below) with their help, and get yourself started on the road to financial independence.

THE PROBLEMS

(1) Inflation is the greatest threat to our financial security. Every plan must be constructed so as to minimize the effects of inflation.

(2) Taxes confiscate income and impede growth, often preventing the achievement of financial security. Every legal effort must be made to minimize taxes.

(3) The habit pattern of earning, spending, saving, and, lastly, investing, guarantees financial failure. Learning to pay oneself first through investments is essential to success.

THE SOLUTION

Development of a professionally managed, balanced financial program is the key to obtaining maximum financial success now and in the future. A balanced financial program requires planning and allocation of resources into all four major areas.

163

Emergency Account	Insurance Account	Investment Account	Distribution Account
Cash	Amount	Diversification	Wills
Hospitalization Insurance	Type	Professional Management	Trusts
Disability Insurance	Balance	Tax Shelters	

THE GENERAL RULES

(1) A balanced program requires adequate resources in all four areas.

(2) The financial components of your plan must be adequate for your individual needs and goals.

(3) Every dollar spent must provide maximum value.

FINANCIAL PLANNING QUESTIONNAIRE

1. Family Data

A. Client's full name _____ Birthdate _____

Street address _____ Social Security number _____

City and state _____ Zip code _____

B. Spouse's first name _____ Birthdate _____

Youngest child _____ Birthdate _____

Child 2 _____ Birthdate _____

Child 3 _____ Birthdate _____

Child 4 _____ Birthdate _____

2. Your Estate and Financial Goals

A. At what age do you plan to retire? _____ What total monthly income do you desire? _____

B. If you were permanently disabled, what would your monthly income needs be? _____

C. In case of your death, what would the immediate cash needs of your family be?

164

(1) Final expenses including taxes _____

(2) Adjustment period expenses _____

(3) Debts _____

(4) Education funds _____

(5) Mortgage reduction _____

(6) Other cash needs _____

D. After these immediate cash needs, what monthly income would be required for your family?

(1) Children at home _____

(2) Widow alone _____

Note: You would want family to continue to live in:

(a) Present home _____

(b) Different home _____

(c) Rent _____

Spouse would work during:

(a) Dependency period _____ Monthly earnings _____

(b) Gap period _____ Monthly earnings _____

(c) For life _____ Monthly earnings _____

3. Capital Assets

	Principal's Property	Spouse's Property	Joint Property	Liquid Asset	Non-Liquid Asset
A. Cash and savings	___	___	___	___	___
B. Home	___	___	___	___	___
C. Other real estate	___	___	___	___	___
D. Stocks, bonds, mutual funds	___	___	___	___	___

E. Personal property ___ ___ ___ ___ ___

F. Business interests ___ ___ ___ ___ ___

G. Corporate, partnership, sole proprietorship ___ ___ ___ ___ ___

H. Mortgages and notes receivable ___ ___ ___ ___ ___

I. Other miscellaneous property ___ ___ ___ ___ ___

J. Non-tax qualified annuity ___ ___ ___ ___ ___

K. Keogh, IRA, TSA ___ ___ ___ ___ ___

L. Trusts on inheritance ___ ___ ___ ___ ___

4. Liabilities

	Principal	Spouse	Joint	To Be Liquidated	Not to Be Liquidated
A. Mortgage on home	___	___	___	___	___
B. Mortgage on other real estate	___	___	___	___	___
C. Notes payable	___	___	___	___	___
D. Current bills	___	___	___	___	___
E. Income taxes payable	___	___	___	___	___
F. Installment indebtedness	___	___	___	___	___
G. Loans on life insurance	___	___	___	___	___
H. Real estate taxes payable	___	___	___	___	___
I. Other indebtedness	___	___	___	___	___

5. Assets Excludable from Principal's Estate

Type of Property	Amount	Owner	Beneficiary
A. Pension plan	————	————	————
B. Profit-sharing plan	————	————	————
C. Life insurance by others	————	————	————
D. Deferred compensation plan	————	————	————
E. Trusts	————	————	————
F. Other	————	————	————

6. Insurance

Policy Type and Number	Face Amount	Owner	Bene-ficiary	Annual Pre-mium	Current Cash Value	Loans	Divi-dends	Cash Value at Retire-ment

A. Client

————	————	————	————	————	————	————	————	————
————	————	————	————	————	————	————	————	————
————	————	————	————	————	————	————	————	————
————	————	————	————	————	————	————	————	————
————	————	————	————	————	————	————	————	————
————	————	————	————	————	————	————	————	————
Totals ————				————	————	————	————	————

B. Family members

————	————	————	————	————	————	————	————	————
————	————	————	————	————	————	————	————	————
————	————	————	————	————	————	————	————	————
Totals ————				————	————	————	————	————

C. Disability income insurance: _____

D. Hospital insurance: _____

7. General Information

	Occupation	Employer	Phone	Annual Income
A. Client	_____	_____	_____	_____
Spouse	_____	_____	_____	_____

B. Do you have wills? _____ Type _____

C. Have you made any gifts? _____ To whom? _____ Amount _____

D. Have you made any charitable bequests? _____ To whom? _____

Amount _____

E. Name of your attorney _____

F. Name of your accountant _____

cA Bibliographical Note

More details on our sources and information can be obtained from the *Congressional Record*, Volume 121, Number 106, for July 8, 1975, available from your U.S. Senator or Representative for only 25 cents. Pages S-11975 to S-11984 are the relevant pages.

The Life Insurance Industry: Hearings before the Subcommittee on Antitrust and Monopoly of the Committee of the Judiciary, United States Senate, Ninety-Third Congress, First Session, February 20, 1973. These are the Hart hearings. You can get most of the results and background information by ordering Volume I for $5.25 from the Superintendent of Documents, U.S. Government Printing Office, Washington, D.C. 20402. Volume III offers some excellent examples of insurance propaganda, particularly the fraud of cash-value insurance. Volumes I through IV cost $5.25, $4.90, $4.35, and $9.20, respectively.

For some chuckles, you might want to look through *Life Insurance Selling*, the magazine for whole-life agents. This isn't sold on newsstands or ordered by libraries, because insurance agents don't want the public reading it, but you can borrow it from independent life insurance agents or financial planners. It contains ads for agents such as "From $7200 to $74,078 in Five Short Years" by selling the whole-life "President's Plan" for the Franklin Life. Obviously, agents don't want customers knowing just how lucrative the business is. Many of these ads are reprinted in Volume I of the Hart hearings.

The only insurance literature that is possibly more amusing than the trade magazines is the report *Life Insurance Companies and the Impact of Inflation: Some Speculations About the Future.* You can write for a copy to the American Council of Life Insurance, 1850 K Street, N.W., Washington, D.C. 20006. We hope that they will send you a copy, but if they don't, it will be interesting to see how they reply to your request.

A Note About the Authors

PETER SPIELMANN was born and raised in Milwaukee, Wisconsin, and graduated from the University of Wisconsin–Milwaukee with honors in psychology. He relocated in Tucson, Arizona, and wrote free-lance news and feature articles for *New Times* newspaper. Returning to Milwaukee a year later, he was hired by the *Bugle-American* "alternative" newspaper, and met Aaron Zelman while doing an article on deceptive practices in the insurance business.

Peter, as a free-lance writer, today works with numerous international, national, and regional publications. He also writes and edits materials selected for publication by the Spielmann/Zelman Publishing Company, a press interested in works that benefit the reader and his society.

AARON ZELMAN was born in Winthrop, Massachusetts, and raised in Tucson, Arizona. He served in both the Navy and Marine Corps as a medic during the Vietnam era, afterward working as a manufacturer's representative for various companies. He then worked as an agent for a large insurance company—until he realized that what was good for the company was not best for the insurance buyer.

Aaron is now an independent insurance agent in Milwaukee, offering complete financial services to his clients. He has been elected to the Board of Directors of the Wisconsin Consumer League, an affiliate of the Consumer Federation of America, and is active in consumer education in Milwaukee. He handles the marketing, research and finances of the Spielmann/Zelman Publishing Company and is also involved in the writing and editing of works selected for publication.

DEAN SHARP has risen through the ranks of law and economics to emerge as America's foremost authority on life insurance reform. He holds three university degrees: an LL.M. in taxation from the New York University Graduate School of Law, a J.D. from Boston University of Law, and a B.S. in economics from the Wharton School of the University of Pennsylvania. A writer, and a member of the bar of the Supreme Court, the Tax Court, Massachusetts, the District of Columbia, as well as of the American and Federal Bar associations, Dean was also an adjunct professor of Law at Georgetown University.

In 1963, after several years of private practice and public service (for the Internal Revenue Service), he became an assistant counsel to the Senate Judiciary Committee's Antitrust and Monopoly Subcommittee, a post he held until December 1974. As such, he was responsible for the subcommittee's investigative and legislative work in the areas of insurance and health care. Dean drafted the late Senator Hart's no-fault automobile insurance bill, as well as Hart's proposed "truth-in-life-insurance" bill. He also conducted extensive public hearings on life insurance, health-care services, and automobile insurance, and compiled twenty-four hearing-record volumes of original research and data. Four of these volumes concern testimony and evidence gathered during the Senate subcommittee's life insurance hearings—evidence so damning that Sharp's work is still bearing fruit today.

Our purpose in writing this book has been to amuse, entertain, outrage, and enlighten the insurance-buying public. What was your reaction? We would like to know, so that we can make necessary changes in future editions of the book. Please write us to let us know how you felt about it. All replies will be given our personal consideration.

Thanks,

PETER SPIELMANN,
AARON ZELMAN,
DEAN SHARP

Spielmann–Zelman
Publishing Co.
P.O. Box 76
Milwaukee, Wisconsin
53201

171